Closing the Education Achievement Gaps for African American Males

Closing the Education Achievement Gaps for African American Males

Edited by Theodore S. Ransaw *and* Richard Majors

Michigan State University Press | *East Lansing*

♾ The paper used in this publication meets the minimum requirements
of ANSI/NISO Z39.48-1992 (R 1997) (Permanence of Paper).

Michigan State University Press
East Lansing, Michigan 48823-5245

Printed and bound in the United States of America.

25 24 23 22 21 20 19 18 17 16   1 2 3 4 5 6 7 8 9 10

LIBRARY OF CONGRESS CATALOGING-IN-PUBLICATION DATA
Closing the education achievement gaps for African American males /
edited by Theodore S. Ransaw and Richard Majors.
pages cm.—(International race and education)
Includes bibliographical references and index.
ISBN 978-1-61186-201-0 (print : alk. paper)—ISBN 978-1-60917-487-3 (pdf)—
ISBN 978-1-62895-262-9 (epub)—ISBN 978-1-62896-262-8 (kindle) 1. African American boys—
Education. 2. African American young men—Education. 3. Academic achievement—
United States. I. Ransaw, Theodore S. II. Majors, Richard.
LC2717.C56 2016
371.829'96073—dc23
2015022472

Book design by Charlie Sharp, Sharp Designs, Lansing, Michigan
Cover design by Shaun Allshouse, www.shaunallshouse.com

Michigan State University Press is a member of the Green Press Initiative and is committed to developing
and encouraging ecologically responsible publishing practices. For more information about the Green
Press Initiative and the use of recycled paper in book publishing, please visit www.greenpressinitiative.org.

Visit Michigan State University Press at www.msupress.org

Contents

Introduction

At this writing, it seems as if there are more programs, conferences, symposiums, panels, initiatives as well as policies about education for African Americans and Black males than ever before. We have the White House's My Brother's Keeper initiative, the Educational Excellence for African Americans initiative, the annual Black Male Development Symposium, the African American Boys Conference, the CUNY annual Black Male Initiative, the annual African American Male Youth Conference, and there is also the National Conference on Educating Black Children that has been in operation for twenty-eight years, just to name a few. However, the problem of education achievement gaps and African American males has been going on for over fifty years (Murphy, 2010). While not specifically about Black males, it is interesting to note that Carter G. Woodson wrote about the same problems that African Americans are experiencing in education in his book *The Mis-Education of the Negro* in 1933, nearly one hundred years ago!

Contemporary authors have not strayed far from this thinking. Dr. Jawanza Kunjufu wrote in 1990 that it appears as if there is a conspiracy to destroy Black boys. The impetus of this thinking stems from the fact that in America, the negative images of Black males are so embedded and pervasive in our culture that they are perceived as violent, unemployed, uneducated, and uneducable (Ransaw, 2014).

Unfavorable perceptions of Black males are so persistent that the way they walk, talk, and even their names can be barriers to them in school (Ransaw, 2013). Some Black males suffer so much from low self-esteem that they doubt the possibility of getting a good education; accordingly, they do not even try to succeed when they come to school (Curnutte, 1998). Woodson so wisely tells us when you "handicap a student by teaching him that his black face is a curse and that his struggle to change his condition is hopeless . . . [that] is the worst sort of lynching" (1990, 2–3).

As a result, many Black males put on a virtual mask of coolness to protect themselves from racial and social oppression. They act cool as a way of defending themselves against myriad ubiquitous inequities in America. This mask is a source of inner strength; a nonviolent, confident, cool form of resistance against oppression (De La Cancela, 1994). De La Cancela (1994) suggests the masklike response to oppression is fabricated to defend against cultural assimilation. Majors and Billson (1992) describe this mask of coolness that is often exemplary of Black males as a *cool pose.*

In Africa, the art of making masks is traditionally handed down from father to son (Lommel, 1970). African masks serve as tools for social communication. Although decorative, African masks typically are adorned with hidden symbols such as spirit animals, star constellations, or celestial mapping. One African snake mask is over fifteen feet tall, and the zig-zag pattern around its border tracks solar orbits of the Sirius star system. Masks also vary in appearance and are subject to interpretation. However, despite their many differences, masks have one thing in common: they reveal something about the person wearing them. When Black males portray themselves with their mask of coolness in the classroom, they are doing more than just being disruptive; they are adopting naturally culturally affirming masculine behavior. This *cool pose* is an art form and can be used as a way to engage Black males in lessons and activities and not as an indicator of when to push them out of the education system.

Take Chicago's Urban Preparatory Academy as a successful example. For three straight years, 100 percent of their students were accepted to colleges (Preston & Wojciechowski, 2012). All of the students at Urban Prep Academy are men of color. Additionally, there are White female teachers who are succeeding in educating Black males (Hardy, 2010). New and innovative trends are showing great promise in the improving the education of Black males. The authors are so confident about this new thought—that there are ideas and approaches that have the potential to close the education achievement of Black males—we have written an entire book about it!

Closing the Education Achievement Gaps for African American Males is a compilation of works of multiple authors from different fields that explore new trends and directions to solve the contemporary problems of educating Black males. Do males and boys have different learning preferences than females? What role does peer pressure play in a Black male's expectations for himself? Is a child's spirit something that teachers can nurture in order to cultivate his desire to stay in school? Can this same motivation translate to success in college? Does attending school largely with other African Americans help or hinder a Black male? How can response to intervention (RTI) plans make a difference for Black males? What roles do academics and family play in the success or hindrance of the Black male athlete? How can teachers create more positive interactions with their Black male students? These are just a few of the items you will find in this book. You will also find handouts throughout as we learn together and from each other.

Chapter and Verse

Additionally, *Closing the Education Achievement Gaps for African American Males* provides eight chapters full of information, callout margins, and tips from the field. We begin with two schools of thought about male learning styles: biological and cultural. We then move into a common problem with African American males of all ages and social economic statuses: peer pressure. Since peer pressure is related to so many things including lack of motivation to go to school, our next chapter covers dropout prevention for African American males in predominantly Black schools and predominantly White schools. Next is a chapter about the necessity and promise of using smartphones to increase engagement and educational outcomes with Black males. The following chapter covers RTI, which, when implemented correctly, holds the potential to keep Black males who should not be in special education out of special education, while the chapter on the Black male athlete details how family support is key to academic success for African American males. Mentorship and increasing educational outcomes is typically synonymous in talking about closing gaps with Black males. However, we provide assessment based practices for those wishing to mentor Black boys. Our final chapter looks at reversing negative expectations as a way to engage Black males. Spread out throughout the chapters are special add-ins and tips that help support classroom implementation of the main ideas.

How to Use This Book

Throughout the volume, you will find emerging trends and directions that relate to African American males in the classroom. Each of the ideas is based on research. All of the chapters highlight major sections in bold. There is a reference section at the end of each chapter in case you would like to do further reading on any of the ideas or suggestions. At the end of the volume you also will find handouts that present exercises, activities, and resources that can be used in the classroom.

REFERENCES

Curnutte, M. (1998). For some Black students, failing is safer: Many who strive to do well often face peers who call them "too White." *Cincinnati Enquirer.*

De La Cancela, V. (1994). "Coolin": The psychosocial communication of African and Latino men. In D. J. Jones (Ed.), *African American males: A critical link in the African American family* (pp. 33–45). New Brunswick: Transaction Publishers.

Hardy, N. (2010). *Portraits of success: Effective White female teachers of Black male middle school students* (Unpublished doctoral dissertation). University of North Carolina at Chapel Hill.

Kunjufu, J. (1990). *Countering the conspiracy to destroy Black boys* (Vol. 3). Chicago: African American Images.

Lommel, A. (1970). *Masks, their meaning and function.* New York: McGraw-Hill.

Majors, R., & Billson, J. M (1992). *Cool pose: The dilemmas of Black manhood in America.* New York: Lexington Books.

Murphy, J. (2010). *The educator's handbook for understanding and closing achievement gaps.* Thousand Oaks, CA: Corwin.

Preston, A., & Wojciechowski, C. (2012). *Threepeat: All urban prep seniors college-bound.* Retrieved from http://www.nbcchicago.com.

Ransaw, T. S. (2013). *The art of being cool: The pursuit of Black masculinity.* Chicago: African American Images.

———. (2014). The good father: African American fathers who positively influence the educational outcomes of their children. *Spectrum: A Journal on Black Men 2*(2), 1–25.

Woodson, C. G. (1990). *The Mis-education of the Negro.* Trenton, NJ: Africa World Press.

Male and Black Male Learning Styles

Theodore S. Ransaw

Presumption should never make us neglect that which appears easy to us, nor despair make us lose courage at the sight of difficulties.

—Benjamin Banneker

The U.S. graduation rates from public high schools are especially low for males, 65 percent, and are even lower for minority males: 55 percent for African Americans and 53 percent for Hispanics (Greene & Winters, 2006). A contributing factor to these poor graduation rates is a lack of reading achievement. While there is no one size fits all to what and how boys prefer to learn, the need to focus on the achievement of boys is evident considering girls outperform boys in almost every related category of reading (OECD, 2006).

Overview

A learning style is both the natural and developmental way that identical instruction is successful or unsuccessful for students (Dunn & Dunn, 1993). Learning style has also been defined as a "complex manner in which, and conditions under which, learners most efficiently and most effectively perceive, process, store, and recall what they are attempting to learn" (James & Blank, 1993, p. 47). Clearly, learning occurs differently for different students.

Gardner (1993) details six different types of learning styles: (1) *linguistic*, the ability to use spoken words, and *logical-mathematical*, inductive and deductive thinking and reasoning abilities, logic, and the use of numbers and abstract pattern recognition; (2) *visual-spatial*, the ability to mentally visualize objects and spatial dimensions; (3) *body-kinesthetic*, the wisdom of the body and the ability to control physical motion; (4) *musical-rhythmic*, the ability to master music as well as rhythms, tones, and beats; (5) *interpersonal*, the ability to communicate effectively with other people and to develop relationships; and (6) *intrapersonal*, the ability to understand one's own emotions, motivations, and inner states of being and capacity for self-reflection. These categorizations seem to apply to both boys and girls. However, this does not mean that gender does not have a place in the way we learn.

In regard to male and female learning styles, there are two main streams of thought, biological and cultural (Ransaw, 2013). The biological stream reports that brains of males and females are just wired differently (Cleveland, 2011). To that point, a research paper from the National Institute of Mental Health in Bethesda, Maryland, asserts that girls are developmentally ahead of boys by at least two years in the early stages. However, the same paper asserts that boys begin to surpass girls by the age of fourteen (Sax, 2006). The point is that boys and girls mature differently, and therefore behave differently, which in turn plays an important role in their learning styles and preferences.

The second school of thought regarding male and female learning is cultural. Being male is a practice that is being re-created under constantly changing social conditions, including resistance by subordinate groups (Wedgwood, 2009) and is not a fixed biological behavior (Bean & Harper, 2007). Put simply, some believe that boys are socialized into gender roles that are more physical than intellectual (McDougal, 2007). Some researchers call this cultural conditioning the boy code (Cleveland, 2011; Pollack, 1998). The boy code is both the formal and informal messages that males receive as to acceptable male behavior in society (Pollack, 1998). These messages, which focus on being tough, independent, and self-resilient, make it difficult for boys to ask for help. While there are gender differences in the way we learn, there are also differences in the way gender and age play a role in the way we learn.

Male Learning Styles

For example, during the developmental stages between nine and seventeen girls tend to become preoccupied with how individual peers view them while boys are more interested in group status (Guyer et al., 2009). Additionally, brain scans reveal that, in general, girls' cerebral cortexes, the area of the brain responsible for memory, attention, thought, and language, are dedicated to verbal functions. For boys, in general, their cerebral cortex is dedicated to spatial awareness. Boys also have less oxytocin and serotonin, hormones that help to bring a sense of calm, than girls do (Zamosky, 2011). However, boys do have higher levels of testosterone and dopamine in their blood, which is known to increase impulse behavior and physical activity (McDougal, 2007). Is it any wonder that boys are characterized as unable to sit still in class?

Research also suggests that girls are more sensitive to sounds and more proficient at fine motor skills than boys (Restak, 1979). Boys, on the other hand, are more visually acute, able to think in three dimensions, and more adept at gross motor skills (Restak, 1979). These fine motor skill assessments—for example, neat handwriting and the ability to cut out small bits of paper with scissors, abilities that are considered benchmarks for early stages of development—are not favorable to young boys. This may be the reason people say that girls develop faster than boys. Gross motor skills, an aptitude more prevalent in young males, is more akin to kinesthetic learning styles.

Kinesthetic Learning Styles

A preference for hands-on multisensory activities is part of the learning style of kinesthetic learners (Davis, 1998). According to Gordon (1998), kinesthetic learners also typically have illegible cursive handwriting, typically stand close when talking, and are poor test takers. Additionally, kinesthetic learners do not like sitting still for long periods of time (Clark, 2010). If you look at the characteristics of male learning styles, they tend to mirror kinesthetic preferences. Males of color tend to prefer kinesthetic learning, especially Black males. However, Black males prefer receiving information both kinesthetically and in other ways.

Black Male Learning Styles

For example, Johnson (2013) asserts that Black male students prefer "more verbal and kinesthetic learning activities" (p. 123). However, McDougal (2007) suggests that Black males prefer receiving information visually. I take these two perspectives as indicators that Black males may prefer information presented to them in a way that helps them see the world so as to adapt to it in ways that are meaningful to them. McDougal (2007) suggests that Black males prefer information that is relatable to the world in which they live. It may be that Black males can project themselves into visual images more readily. Portrayals of Black men are rarely based on perceptions of them as active participants, so they may be more adept and practiced at decoding visual images and finding heuristic value relative and meaningful to their lives. Hyperawareness of race is almost inevitable for people of color who live in a world and attend school in buildings where they are measured against racial markers. In the United States, Whiteness is the measure of standards. For example, there is an achievement gap between African Americans and Latinos. No one ever talks about the overrepresentation of White students in advanced and college preparatory classes or the achievement gap between Asians and Whites.

Noguera (2006) attests that from first grade until college, Black students feel their very humanity is under scrutiny if they make any academically related mistakes. In particular Black male students are also especially conscious of looking foolish or dumb in school (Majors & Billson, 1992). Some researchers feel that this hyperawareness of the appearance of competence may be a result of withdrawing from schooling because of unequal treatment or low expectations (Graham, Taylor, & Hudley, 1998), or even negative perceptions of academic ability by their teachers (Osborne, 1999). Researchers assert that disinterest in school by Black males is assumed to be caused by low intellectual ability (Downey & Pribesh, 2004). However, New Orleans Principal Booker champions another idea that Black male students understand and value education but feel disconnected from schooling, and that the feeling of belonging is crucial for academic success (WDSU News, 2012). This finding is supported by additional research that indicates Black male students do well in classroom discussions that are inclusive and center on Black culture while affirming their identity (Boykin & Bailey, 2000). However, when Black males use cultural markers such as nonstandard English, they are perceived as outsiders and aggressive (Delphit, 1995). Interpreting alternative cultural identifiers, including different language used, as deviant is not uncommon for teachers who walk in life and step into a classroom unfamiliar with African American norms (Durodoye & Hildreth, 1995). Nor is it uncommon for teachers to view African American culture as deficient since it is expressed differently than White values, beliefs, and behaviors (Durodoye & Hildreth, 1995). Being unaware of African American culture may be why any resistance to White cultural norms by Black students results in negative perceptions of academic ability (Sankofa et al., 2005), while the closer to White norms of body language and emotions students of color come, the more likely they are perceived as self-disciplined and acceptable (Delpit, 1995). Racial solidarity for communal support in the classroom may be why African American students prefer to work in groups (Lee, 2000). Resistance to cultural assimilation such as "talking White" may be a reaction to the unconscious fear of losing classroom solidarity among African Americans (Comer & Poussaint, 1992).

Many high-achieving Black students report being stigmatized as a sell-out when they start to outpace their peers (Curnutte, 1998). Consequently, high-achieving Black male students are more likely *not* to prefer working in groups (McDougal, 2007). Additionally, Black male students who have consistently high academic scores prefer to study in the afternoon, and they preferred studying with lots of light (McDougal, 2007). Lastly, having a dedicated place to study in the home is an indicator of academic success for Black males (McDougal, 2007). Having a specific place in the house for academics is a causal relationship to parental involvement.

Wrap-up

When it comes to learning style preferences, it is important to remember three facts. The first is that "learning styles are neither good nor bad, they simply exist" (Cozens, 1999, p. 6). Second, not all students are the same, even within a specific gendered or ethnic group. Therefore, teachers may find more success if they pay attention to individual learning preferences as much as they can (Cozens, 1999). Finally, students, especially when they are young, "need to be competent in all learning styles, auditory, visual, tactile, and kinesthetic" (Cozens, 1999, p. 8). This is called "style shift" where teachers, "achieve a balance between teaching strategies and the students' unique learning styles. Thus, teachers are encouraged to adjust their teaching strategies in light of the different learning styles of the students" (Suleiman, 1995, p. 3).

Regardless of gender, what may be an effective learning style for some may not be an effective learning style for others (Dunn & Dunn, 1993). It is important for us all to remember that "learning styles are neither good nor bad, they simply exist" (Cozens, 1999, p. 6) and to recognize individual learning differences more so than entire group characteristics (Cozens, 1999).

REFERENCES

Akbar, N. (1985). *The community of self.* Tallahassee, FL: Mind Productions and Associates.

Allen, B. A., & Boykin, A. W. (1992). African-American children and the educational process: Alleviating cultural discontinuity through prescriptive pedagogy. *School Psychology Review* *21*, 586–596.

Amodeo, L. B., & Brown, D. (1986). Students from Mexico in U.S. school. *Educational Horizons* *64*, 192–196.

Banks, J. A., & McGee-Banks, C. A. (Eds.). (2004). *Handbook of research on multicultural education* (2nd ed.). San Francisco: Jossey-Bass.

Bean, T., & Harper, H. (2007). Reading men differently: Alternative portrayals of masculinity in contemporary young adult fiction. *Reading Psychology 28*(1), 11–30.

Boykin, A. W. (1983). The academic task performance and Afro-American children. In J. T. Spence (Ed.), *Achievement and achievement motives: Psychological and sociological approaches* (pp. 324–371). San Francisco: W. H. Freeman.

Boykin, A. W., & Bailey, C. (2000). *The role of cultural factors in school relevant cognitive functioning: Synthesis of findings on cultural contexts, cultural orientations and individual differences (Report 42).* Washington, DC, and Baltimore, MD: Howard University and Johns Hopkins University, Center for Research on the Education of Students Placed at Risk (CRESPAR).

Boynton, L. F. M. (1994). *The relationship between congruent student and parent learning style preferences and homework performance of middle school students in regular and resource classes* (Unpublished doctoral dissertation). La Sierra University, Riverside, CA.

Bristow, B. (2000). *The effects of hands-on instruction on 6th grade student understanding of electricity and magnetism* (Unpublished master's thesis). Texas Woman's University, Denton, TX.

Clark, R. C. (2010). Evidence-based training methods: A guide for training professionals. Alexandria, VA: ASTD Press.

Cleveland, K. P. (2011). *Teaching boys who struggle in school: Strategies that turn underachievers into successful learners.* Alexandria, VA: ASCD.

Cohen, R. A. (1969). Conceptual styles, cultural conflict, and nonverbal tests of intelligence. *American Anthropologist 71*, 828–856.

Comer, J. P., & Poussaint, A. P. (1992). *Raising Black children: Two leading psychiatrists confront the educational, social, and emotional problems facing Black children.* New York: Plume.

Cozens, G. A. (1999). *An investigation of the learning styles of ninth-grade public school students: Black and White, male and female, general level and gifted/magnet* (Unpublished doctoral dissertation). University of Georgia, Athens.

Curnutte, M. (1988). For some Black students, failing is safer: Many who strive to do well often face peers who call them "too White." *Cincinnati Enquirer.*

Davis, O. L., Jr. (1998). Beyond beginnings: From "hands-on" to "minds-on." *Journal of Curriculum and Supervision 13*, 119–122.

Delpit, L. (1995). *Other people's children: Cultural conflict in the classroom.* New York: The New Press.

Downey & Pribesh, 2004. When race matters: Teachers' evaluations of students' classroom behavior. *Sociology of Education 77*(4), 267–282.

Dunn, R. S., & Dunn, K. J. (1993). *Teaching secondary students through their individual learning styles: Practical approaches for grades 7–12.* Boston: Allyn and Bacon.

Durodoye, B., & Hildreth, B. (1995). Learning styles and the African American student. *Education 116*(2), 241.

Ewing, N. J., & Yong, F. (1992). A comparative study of the learning style preferences among gifted African-American, Mexican-American and American-born Chinese middle grade students. *Roeper Review 14*, 120–123.

Gardner, H. (1993). *Multiple intelligences: The theory in practice.* New York: Basic.

Gordon, H. R. (1998). *Identifying learning styles.* ERIC: ED424287. Paper presented at the Annual Summer Workshop for Beginning Vocational Education Teachers. MV: Montgomery.

Graham, S., Taylor, A., & Hudley, C. (1998). Exploring achievement among ethnic minority early adolescents. *Journal of Educational Psychology 90*, 606–620.

Green, R. S. (1995). *The preferred learning styles of four African-American males: A case study analysis* (Unpublished doctoral dissertation). Indiana University, Bloomington.

Greene, J. P., & Winters, M. A. (2006). *Leaving boys behind: Public high school graduation rates.* University of Arkansas Education Working Paper Archive.

Guyer, A. E., McClure-Tone, E. B., Shiffrin, N. D., Pine, D. S., & Nelson, E. E. (2009). Probing the neural correlates of anticipated peer evaluation in adolescence. *Child Development 80*, 1000–1015.

Herring, R. L. (2014). *The effects of kinesthetic teaching strategies on student academic achievement in science* (Unpublished doctoral dissertation). Fielding Graduate Institute.

Hilliard, A. G. (1998). *SBA: The reawakening of the African mind.* Gainesville, FL: Makare Publishing.

Jackson-Allen, J., & Christenberry, N. J. (1994). *Learning style preferences of low- and high-achieving young African-American males.* Paper presented at Mid-South Educational Research Association, Nashville, TN.

Jacobs, R. L. (1987). *An investigation of the learning style differences among Afro-American and Euro-American high, average, and low achievers* (Unpublished doctoral dissertation). Vanderbilt University George Peabody College, Nashville.

James, W. B., & Blank, W. E. (1993). Review and critique of available learning-style instruments for adults. *New Directions for Adult and Continuing Education*, no. 59, 47–57.

Johnson, K. C. (2013). *Teacher and parent perceptions of classroom experiences of African American male students in a high school alternative program* (Unpublished doctoral dissertation). Pepperdine University, Malibu, CA.

Kagan, S. (1986). Cooperative learning and sociocultural factors in schooling. In California Department of Education (Ed.), *Beyond language: Social and cultural factors in schooling language minority students* (pp. 231–298). Los Angeles: Evaluation, Dissemination and Assessment Center, California State University.

Kambon, K. K. (2005). *Cultural misorientation: The greatest threat to the survival of the Black race in the 21st century.* Tallahassee, FL: Nubian Nation Publications.

Kauchak, D. P., & Eggen, P. D. (2003). *Learning and teaching: Research based methods* (4th ed.). Boston: Allyn and Bacon.

Keefe, J. W. (1979). Learning style: An overview. In O. B. Kiernan (Ed.), *Student learning styles: Diagnosing and prescribing programs* (pp. 1–17). Reston, VA: National Association of Secondary School Principals.

Klavas, A. (1994). Learning style program boosts achievement and test scores. *The Clearing House 67*(3), 149–151.

Lee, C. D. (2000). Signifying in the zone of proximal development. In C. D. Lee & P. Smagorinsky (Eds.), *Vygotskian perspectives on literacy research: Constructing meaning through collaborative inquiry*, 191–225. New York: Cambridge University Press.

Madhere, S. (1999). *Psychology, pedagogy, and talent cultivation.* Paper presented at the Conference on Psychology and Caribbean Development, University of the West Indies at Mona.

Majors, R., & Billson, J. M. (1992). *Cool pose: The dilemmas of Black manhood in America.* New York: Lexington Books.

Martin, D., Martin, M., Gibson, S. S., & Wilkins, J. (2007). Increasing prosocial behavior and academic achievement among adolescent African American males. *Adolescence 42*(168), 689–698.

Martinez, R., & Dukes, R. L. (1987). Race, gender and self-esteem among youth. *Hispanic Journal of Behavioral Sciences 9*, 427–443.

Mason, S. M. (2013). *The school leader's role with response to intervention with African American males in urban school districts* (Unpublished doctoral dissertation). Walden University.

Mazama, A. (Ed.). 2003. *The Afrocentric paradigm.* Trenton, NJ: Africa World Press.

McDougal, S. (2007). *An Afrocentric analysis of teacher/student style congruency and high school Black male achievement levels* (Unpublished doctoral dissertation). Temple University, Philadelphia, PA.

Noguera, P. (2006). How Listening to Students can Help High Schools to Improve. *Theory Into Practice 46*(3), 205–2011.

OECD (Organization of Economic Cooperation and Development). (2006). *Education at a glance 2006: OECD indicators.* OECD Publishing.

Osborne, J. (1999). Unraveling the underachievement among African American boys from identification with academic perspective. *Journal of Negro Education, 68*, 555–565.

Park, C. C. (1997). Learning style preferences of Asian American (Chinese, Filipino, Korean, and Vietnamese) students in secondary schools. *Equity & Excellence in Education 30*(2), 68–77.

———. (2001). Learning style preferences of Armenian, African, Hispanic, Hmong, Korean, Mexican, and Anglo students in American secondary schools. *Learning Environments Research 4*, 175–191.

Pollack, William S. (1999). *Real boys: Rescuing our sons from the myths of boyhood.* New York: Henry Holt & Company.

Ransaw, T. S. (2013). *The art of being cool: The pursuit of Black masculinity.* Chicago: African American Images.

Restak, R. M. (1979). The other differences between boys and girls. In O. B. Kiernan (Ed.), *Student learning styles: Diagnosing and prescribing programs* (pp. 75–80). Reston, VA: National Association of Secondary School Principals.

Sankofa, B. M., Hurley, E. A., Allen, B. A., & Boykin, A. W. (2005). Cultural expression and Black students' attitudes toward high achievers. *The Journal of Psychology: Interdisciplinary & Applied, 139*(3), 247–259.

Sax, L. (2007). *Boys adrift: The five factors driving the growing epidemic of unmotivated boys and underachieving young men.* New York: Basic Books.

Searson, R., & Dunn, R. (2001). The learning style teaching model. *Science and Children 38*(5), 22–26.

Suleiman, M. F. (1995). *Achieving congruence between learning and teaching styles in linguistically diverse environments.* Paper presented at the Annual Meeting of the National Social Science Conference, San Diego, CA.

Vasquez, J. (1990). Teaching to the Distinctive Traits of Minority Students. *The Clearing House* 63(7), 299–304.

WDSU News. (2012). *African-American male teacher a vanishing phenomenon, experts say 2 percent of nation's teachers are African American men.* WDSU.com, April 27, 2012.

Wedgwood, N. (2009). Connell's theory of masculinity: Its origins and influences on the study of Gender. *Journal of Gender Studies* 18(4), 329–339.

Williams, G. (1989). *A study of the learning styles of urban Black middle school learning disabled and non-learning disabled students* (Unpublished doctoral dissertation). Southern Illinois University, Carbondale.

Willis, M. G. (1989). Learning styles of African American children: A review of the literature and interventions. *Journal of Black Psychology* 16(1), 47–65.

Zamosky, L. (2011). How boys and girls learn differently. *WebMD.* Retrieved from http://www.webmd.com.

Black Males, Peer Pressure, and High Expectations

Theodore S. Ransaw and Robert L. Green

The thought of the inferiority of the Negro is drilled into him in almost every class he enters and in almost every book he studies.

—Carter G. Woodson

It was over thirty years ago that Dr. Jawanza Kunjufu published his seminal volume regarding a common phenomenon among African American males in the classroom: *To Be Popular or Smart* (Kunjufu, 1988). In the introduction written by basketball legend Karim Abdul-Jabbar, Abdul-Jabbar outlines his adolescent experience not just as an athlete, but about how he was treated by his peers as an academically inclined student. Abdul-Jabbar describes his experience in schooling as a place where he learned early how to deal with Blacks who made fun of him for being smart while simultaneously being showcased by White educators as a Black boy who could "speak well" (Abdul-Jabbar in Kunjufu, 1988). Social class and racial identification are two important factors for Blacks in the United States.

For African American youth of low socioeconomic status (SES), who fear losing communal and ethnic solidarity to Blacks who are moving into the middle class, insults related to selling out are often unconscious reactions to possible abandonment (Comer & Poussaint 1992). Sticking together based on a common racial identity is especially important for African American students who are bused into White schools in White neighborhoods. As the Black middle class continues to grow and to move into the suburbs, many positive role models who have the ability to transmit social capital in the form of educational outcomes move also. This is why the success of the few African Americans who are academically successful make those who are not feel even more like failures (Comer & Poussaint 1992). Add the fact that both Blacks and Whites reinforce success for athleticism, and you have yet another impetus for African American males to gravitate toward sports for cultural affirmation and personal validation. Not all African American males can successfully balance their social capital and educational capital as well as Abdul-Jabbar.

It is also important to note that peer pressure related to academic achievement and African American students is not just a phenomena related to low SES. In fact, peer pressure can be more influential than ethnicity, gender, or income (Johnson, 2000). Ogbu's (2008) research attests that for middle-/upper-class African Americans, peer pressure and educational outcomes have a direct correlation. In the example above about Karim Abdul-Jabbar, Abdul-Jabbar was attending a private school when he was made to feel like the "other."

The following serves as a brief overview of research surrounding African American males in regards to helping them deal with peer pressure. Starting with a background about self-esteem and peer pressure, this work provides insight into how peer pressure places Black males within a unique space within American classrooms.

Literature Review

To begin, it is important to remember that peer pressure can be both negative *and* positive. Negative peer pressure has been associated with risk-taking behavior, substance abuse, and low academic achievement. However, students who spend time among peer groups who are academically inclined but who do not come from families who stress academics tend to get better grades (Peer pressure, 2014). In other words, peer pressure can influence student outcomes both positively and negatively.

This is especially troubling to Black students who seem to get negative peer pressure from both Black and White students when it comes to academic performance. So much so that doing well in school seems to be reserved for White students only. Both African American and Hispanic fourth and eighth graders say that their friends make fun of them when they do well in school (Johnson, 2000). Additionally, higher grades translate to more friends with White teens but fewer friends for African American and Latino youth (Page, 2005). In fact, speaking standard English or reading a book has been shown to be associated with "acting White" (Page, 2005). The fear of the acting White perspective asserts that African Americans reject academics and studiousness because acting smart translates to oppositional culture and acting White (Ogbu, 2008). Ogbu (2008) also suggests that societal and school discrimination instrumental community factors, such as perceptions of lack of jobs, *and* Black oppositional culture are three necessary interrelated factors related to peer pressure and Black students' success.

While all high academic achieving students are subject to teasing by their peers, for African American students academic achievement can be viewed as selling out (Curnutte, 2008). In fact, negative peer pressure is the number one barrier to academic achievement for African American students (Curnutte, 2008). Fordham (1996) agrees, asserting that the fear of being ostracized from negative peer pressure influences many African American students to underachieve.

Curnutte (2008) also suggests that acting White is about not only the way one talks in school but also participation in extracurricular activities such as band and theater. Author Walter Dean Myer said he used to put his school books in brown paper lunch bags to avoid stigma from being perceived as smart. Avoiding perceptions of studiousness in an effort to fit in is also a matter of survival from being bullied (Frosh, Phoenix, & Pattman, 2002). Similar to fitting in, being socially accommodating has particular significance for Black males.

Social accommodation for African American males is so high they can internalize their frustration until it becomes a barely hidden rage. However, this leads some African American male adolescents who cope by suppressing their anger to have significantly fewer close friends and family members to talk to about their personal problems and exacerbates feelings of isolation from their peers (Johnson & Greene, 1991). Brown (2004) asserts this is a significant factor during adolescence, a period where less time is spent with parents and more time is spent with friends, and peer relationships become more complex. Peer influence can operate in at least four ways: (1) direct peer pressure, (2) indirect peer modeling, (3) normative regulation, and (4) structured opportunities (Brown, 2004). This peer effect starts around fourth grade when classrooms begin to move from having one primary teacher and wanes by eighth grade as students become more self-actualized (Johnson, 2000). Fourth grade is so crucial to academic success and positive life outcomes that two-thirds of students who cannot read by the fourth grade will end up in jail or on welfare (Begin to Read, 2015).

In addition to barriers that many of us had already assumed, such as family structure and education opportunities, Williams (2002) also suggests that lack of appropriate self-esteem/self-confidence are also barriers to closing the achievement gap between elementary African American students and White students. According to a survey by Ohio State University, even among African American students in high school negative peer pressure is the number one obstacle for academic achievement (as reported by Curnutte, 2008). The key to success for college-minded African American students is to maintain friendships with peers with similar goals and to avoid negative peers and other bad influences (Curnutte, 2008).

While our focus in this chapter is peer pressure, self-efficacy is highly related to peer pressure. Student self-efficacy can influence everything from problem solving and decision making to the likelihood of having high expectations (Chemers, Hu, & Garcia, 2001). Self-efficacy even influences student outcomes such as resiliency, aspirations, and performance (Chemers, Hu, & Garcia, 2001). Classroom practices affect not only behavioral strategies but perception of student ability as well.

"Teacher perceptions of the male students' self-efficacy for reading and writing may be different than their perception of their female students' self-efficacy for reading and writing" (Corkett, Hatt, & Benevides, 2011, p. 93). A gender-biased view has particular influence not only for males, but especially for African American males who experience negative perceptions as both individuals and as a group. Students as early as grade three begin to look at the achievement rate of their peers, which can influence self-efficacy (Chemers, Hu, & Garcia, 2001). If other students seem to be performing well and the one observing is not, than self-efficacy may decrease for the observer. This is likely to be true especially if the well-performing students are of a different ethnicity than the lower-performing student. An efficacious teacher notices students' feelings of self-worth and beliefs in their abilities and uses those observations constructively.

Theoretical Framework

The following solutions to helping Black students avoid aspects of negative academic peer pressure and embrace supports from positive academic peer pressure are based on two theoretical frameworks. The first is the African American Identity Model comprised of pre-encounter, encounter, immersion/emersion, internalization, and internalization/commitment (Cross & Strauss, 1998). The second is Treynor's (2009) identity shift effect where peer pressure can make an individual conform to a group norm to ameliorate negative feelings related to the internal conflict of loss of identity by adopting the standards of the group as one's own new identity.

In an effort to provide helpful approaches to improving educational outcomes through supportive measures that counter negative peer pressure, we have provided some research-based suggestions about dealing with peer pressure. The appendix also provides some tools, like the "Teachers of Students of Color Self-Efficacy Survey" handout, that have been used in professional development session to bolster self-esteem.

Solutions for Preventing Negative Peer Pressure

What Parents Can Do

- Parents can build their child's self-esteem and racial pride by teaching them the wide scope of Black achievement in the United States and other countries.
- Parents can arrange to have their children associate and play with children from other families who place a high value on education and achievement.
- Parents can set a positive example by getting involved in their children's schools.
- Parents can celebrate Kwanzaa and other Black cultural events that emphasize personal and community excellence.
- Parents can encourage their children to confide in a teacher, minister, or mentor if they are experiencing harassment at school because of their outstanding academic performance if they are not immediately available (Curnutte, 2008).

Use Affirmations

Members of the experimental group in a study by Cohen et al. (2006) were asked to choose one value that was important to them and write a paragraph describing why they cherished the value. The control group students focused on values held by others. Students were not aware that the assignment involved issues related to race and stereotype but viewed the exercise as a normal classroom assignment. This self-affirmation exercise allowed students to reaffirm their beliefs and their own personal identity. Because the exercise did not focus on testing and the stress associated with the negative stereotype threat phenomenon, African American students in the experimental group improved throughout the school year. Cohen et al. indicated that as a result of this psychological intervention, African American students in the experimental group had higher end-of-year grades compared to those in the control group (Cohen et al., 2006, p. 1309).

Continuous and Sustained Mentorship

Effective mentoring is a combination of longitudinal support for both the mentee and the mentor with measurable goals and objectives, which in turn foster and encourage leadership. Most mentorship experiences fail because of a mismatch between the expertise of the mentor and the needs of the mentee, the structure of the relationship between the mentor and mentee in regard to the transmission of information, and a failure to establish a systematic long-term method for engagement (Hilley, 2010). In short, mentorship requires structured leadership.

Mentoring also requires presence and consistency (Ford, Harris, & Schuerger, 1993). Mentor relationships typically deteriorate because mentors fail to commit to the time and effort needed to make a difference (National Urban League, 1992). In addition to understanding the value of participation outcomes, mentors need to be aware of participation competence expectancy and participation outcome expectancy (Ford, Harris, & Schuerger, 1993).

In addition Clark (1995) asserts that mentors must help mentees create a plan of action or "future" plan, know all relevant support services such as campus counselors, health groups, or other support services, and have an awareness of written and unwritten rules pertinent to academic success. This includes knowing how to negotiate bureaucracy, how to build and establish allies, and how to teach mentees how to read and transmit social cues. It is also helpful to facilitate campus tours, library tours, or classroom visits, go to lunch with mentees, and make encouraging phone calls (Clark, 1995) or text messages.

Positive Peer Support

Resiliency is the positive adaptation to adverse circumstances (Luthar, 2006). The period of adolescence is traumatic for most students, but especially so for minority girls who are often bombarded with mixed messages from peer pressure, and that encourages them to embrace and experiment with their sexuality while the media simultaneously rejects ethnic-looking body types. To be fair, the media is not to blame for all problems behind negative self-image concepts of young Black women. However, due to the image identity influences of the mass media, girls are left with two choices: to be a bad girl who strives to fit in and embrace unrealistic body ideals, or to be a bad girl and rebel with violence, aggression, or indiscriminate sex (Kilbourne, 1999). The ability to be resilient is salient for Black girls since school delinquency and self-concept are related to them more so than White girls (Datesman, Scarpitti, & Stephenson, 1975).

Peer Groups

Because of social conditioning, African American students are more likely to seek help from small cooperative groups where they are comfortable challenging explanations, requesting justifications, and being supported with a challenging engagement (Nelson-Le Gall & Jones, 1991). African American students who are high achievers typically do so as members of peer groups (Peer pressure, 2014).

Have High Expectations

High future expectations are an indicator of resilience (Slaughter-Defoe & Rubin, 2001; Wyman et al., 1993). Virginia Beach City Public School research states that teacher expectations are factors contributing to achievement gaps of African American males (White, 2009) while high-performing schools tend to have high standards and expectations for all students (Henderson & Mapp, 2002). Kunjufu (2002) suggests in his book *Black Students, Middle Class Teachers* that altering the expectations of Black males is one of the crucial keys to helping them overcome the academic achievement gap (Green, 2009).

Believe in Yourself

Well-intentioned teachers can feel as if they cannot reach their Black male students, lose hope, and tend to focus more on students that look and act more like them. "You know if I had someone to work with C [a young African American] it would free me up to help the kids that are right there on the edge that need help" (Blanca in Alexander, 2009, p. 108). However, there is no research that suggests only Black teachers can teach Black students (Ladson-Billings, 2005; Tatum, 2005). Surprisingly, we do not have to separate culture from academic rigor. It's a lot more helpful to focus on being a good teacher. Good teachers can have a positive effect on minority students (Singham, 2003).

Don't Be Afraid of Rigor

In fact there is even a rigor/relevance framework based on six components: (1) remember, (2) understand, (3) apply, (4) analyze, (5) evaluate, and (6) synthesize (Paulson, 2008). The best way to assist students with rigor is to help them use these six steps in a way that helps them to apply what they are learning in ways that are meaningful in their lives and by connecting their education into frameworks they can use in their professional futures.

REFERENCES

Alexander, D. R. (2009). *What's so special about special education? A critical study of white general education teachers' perceptions regarding the referrals of African American students for special education services.* (Unpublished doctoral dissertation). Texas A&M University.

Begin to Read. (2015). Literacy statistics. Retrieved at: http://begintoread.com.

Brown, B. B. (2004). Adolescents' relationships with peers. In R. M. Lerner & L. Steinberg (Eds.), *Handbook of adolescent psychology* (2nd ed.) (pp. 363–394). Hoboken, NJ: Wiley.

Chambers, S. M., & Hardy, J. C. (2005). Length of time in student teaching: Effects on classroom control orientation and self-efficacy beliefs. *Educational Research Quarterly* 28(3), 3–9.

Chemers, M. M., Hu, L., & Garcia, B. F. (2001). Academic self-efficacy and first-year college student performance and adjustment. *Journal of Educational Psychology* 93(1), 55–64.

Clark, C. (1995). Innovations in the mentoring process. *Equity and Excellence in Education* 28(2), 65–68.

Cohen, G. L, Garcia, J., Apfel, N., & Master, A. (2006). Reducing the racial achievement gap: A social-psychological intervention. *Science 313*, 1307–1310.

Comer, J. P., & Poussaint, A. P. (1992). *Raising Black children: Two leading psychiatrists confront the educational, social and emotional problems facing Black children.* New York: Plume.

Corkett, J., Hatt, B., & Benevides, T. (2011). Student and teacher self-efficacy and the connection to reading and writing. *Canadian Journal of Education 34*(1), 65–98.

Cross, W. E., & Strauss, L. (1998). The everyday functions of African American identity. In J. K. Swim & C. Stangor (Eds.), *Prejudice: The target's perspective* (pp. 267–279). San Diego: Academic Press.

Curnutte, M. (2008). For some Black students, failing is safer: Many who strive to do well often face peers who call them "too White." *Cincinnati Enquirer.*

Datesman, S. K., Scarpitti, F. R., & Stephenson, R. M. (1975). Female delinquency: An application of self and opportunity theories. *Journal of Research in Crime and Delinquency 12*, 107–123.

Ford, D. Y., Harris, J. J., III, & Schuerger, J. M. (1993). Racial identity development among gifted Black students: Counseling issues and concerns. *Journal of Counseling and Development 71*, 409–417.

Fordham, S. (1996). *Blacked out: Dilemmas of race, identity, and success at Capital High.* Chicago: University of Chicago Press.

Frosh, S., Phoenix, A., & Pattman, R. (2002). *Young masculinities: Understanding boys in contemporary society.* Basingstoke: Palgrave.

Green, R. L. (Ed.). (2009). *Expectations in education: Readings on high expectations, effective teaching, and student achievement.* Columbus, OH: SRA/McGraw Hill.

Henderson, A. T., & Mapp, K. L. (2002). *A new wave of evidence: The impact of school, family, and community connections on student achievement: Annual synthesis 2002.* Austin, TX: National Center for Family and Community Connections with Schools.

Hilley, J. (2010). The current mentorship model is broken. Retrieved from http://www. articlesbase.com.

Hoxby, C., & Turner, S. (2013). *Expanding college opportunities for high-achieving, low income students.* Stanford Institute for Economic Policy Research Paper No. 12-014.

Johnson, E. H., & Greene, A. (1991). The relationship between suppressed anger and psychosocial distress in African American male adolescents. *Journal of Black Psychology 18*(1), 47–65.

Johnson, K. A. (2000). *The peer effect on academic achievement among public elementary students.* Washington, DC: Heritage Foundation.

Kilbourne, J. (1999). *Can't buy my love: How advertising changes the way we think and feel.* New York: Touchstone.

Kunjufu, J. (1988). *To be popular or smart: The Black peer group.* Chicago: African American Images.

————. (2002). *Black students, middle class teachers.* Chicago: African American Images.

Ladson-Billings, G. (1995). But that's just good teaching! The case for culturally relevant pedagogy. *Theory into Practice 34*, 159–165.

Luthar, S. (2006). Resilience in development: A synthesis of research across five decades. In D. Cicchetti & D. J. Cohen (Eds.), *Developmental psychopathology*, Vol. 3: *Risk, disorder, and adaptation* (2nd ed.) (pp. 739–795). Hoboken, NJ: John Wiley.

McPhee, L. (Writer & Director). (1995). Dying to be thin [Television series episode]. In P. Apsell (Producer), *Nova.* PBS.

National Urban League. (1992). *Mentoring young Black males: An overview.* New York: National Urban League.

Nelson-Le Gall, S., & Jones, E. (1991). Classroom help-seeking behavior of African American children. *Education and Urban Society 24(1)*, 27–40.

Ogbu, J. U. (2008). *Minority status, oppositional culture, & schooling.* New York: Routledge.

Page, C. (2005). *Black peer pressure and acting White* [radio broadcast]. E. Gordon [host]. National Public Radio, July 18.

Paulson, M. (2008). *Best teaching practices for rigor in learning.* Retrieved from https://suite101. com/a/rigor-in-the-classroom-a8.

Peer pressure. (2014). At Faqs.org. Retrieved from http://www.faqs.org/health/topics/76/Peer-pressure.html.

Singham, M. (2003). The achievement gap: Myths and reality. *Phi Delta Kappan 84*, 586–591.

Slaughter-Defoe, D. T., & Rubin, H. H. (2001). A longitudinal case study of Head Start eligible children: Implications for urban education. *Educational Psychologist 36*, 31–44.

Steele, C. M (2004). A threat in the air: How stereotypes shape intellectual identity and performance. In J. A. Banks & C. A. McGee-Banks (Eds.), *Handbook of research on multicultural education (2nd ed.)*, 682–688. San Francisco: Jossey-Bass.

Tatum, A. W. (2005). *Teaching reading to Black adolescent males: Closing the achievement gap.* Portland, ME: Stenhouse.

Treynor, W. (2009). *Towards a general theory of social psychology: Understanding human cruelty, human misery, and, perhaps, a remedy (a theory of the socialization process).* Redondo Beach, CA: Euphoria Press.

Valencia, R. (Ed.). (1997). *The evolution of deficit thinking: Educational thought and practice.* Briston, PA: Falmer Press.

White, H. E. (2009). *Increasing the achievement of African American males.* Report from the Department of Research, Evaluation, and Assessment 3. Virginia Beach: Department of

Research Evaluation and Assessment.

Williams, G. J. (2002). *Perceptions of Black male students and their parents about the academic achievement gap between Black and White students at the elementary school level* (Unpublished doctoral dissertation). University of Massachusetts–Amherst.

Wyman, P. A., Cowen, E. L., Work, W. C., & Kerley, J. H. (1993). The role of children's future expectations in self-system functioning and adjustment to life-stress: A prospective study of urban at-risk children. *Development and Psychopathology 5*, 649–661.

Understanding the Superintendent's Dropout Challenge

Challenges and Successes between Schools with Low vs. High Percentages of African American Young Men (of Promise)

Jonathan J. Doll

Human progress is neither automatic nor inevitable. . . . Every step toward the goal of justice requires sacrifice, suffering, and struggle; the tireless exertions and passionate concern of dedicated individuals.

—Martin Luther King Jr.

It's the dawn of a new day for African American male students on the road to becoming men of promise. Opportunities are increasing and support is growing for this important part of American society. In recent news, the national initiative My Brother's Keeper is expanding in its second year of creating programs to support African American male students as they progress through our educational system; in addition, more and more organizations are signing on in support (Rich, 2014). Still, it's important to remember that as Howard University professor Dr. Ivory Toldson powerfully shared, an apology is due (Ford, 2013). The American public and media have often slanted the story of African American success incorrectly, overemphasizing problems and not showing successes. As an example of this from Toldson's research, college access by African American males has been understated in profound ways that miss the bold truth that 1.3 million African American men attend college annually in the United States—much more than the 840,000 who are tragically in prisons (National Public Radio, 2013).

The flip side of the successes of African American men in universities, and the opportunities therein, can be understood through the lens of dropout—a national problem. These are the students whose options are cut short because of a surplus of challenges, combined with a lack of support, lack of mentors, or lack of internal ambition to guide them on the way of educational success. Change can come in many ways, but my research has focused on how mentoring of both students and adults can bring renewal to old systems and nurture people in creating or reinforcing new pathways.

Indeed, dropout is an opportunity killer. The 514,238 students (3.4 percent) who drop out annually in the United States will find significantly lower wage opportunities, higher rates of unemployment, more frequent criminal activity, and a greater sense of loss in the society around them (NCES, 2013). In Michigan, 19.5 percent of dropouts are African Americans, compared to the state rate of 11 percent (MI School Data, 2014). On the positive side, general equivalency diploma (GED) programs are ubiquitous, but the problems associated with dropout often drain the strength of young people, indenturing them to a society that wants them to work for low pay or no pay at all. Between 74 and 81 percent of the dropouts themselves report that graduating would have been vital to their success, and they would change things if they had a second chance (Bridgeland, Dilulio, & Morison, 2006). More, African American young men from focus groups conducted in twenty-eight of Michigan's lower performing schools expressed that they came to school to learn and had aspirations for college despite living within close proximity to crime, violence, poverty, and in some cases overt racism (Borden-Conyers, 2014). Yet they could often see the light at the end of the tunnel and the need to create positive change in their lifetime.

Still, as tragic as this story seems, we have to focus on solutions. The work of dropout prevention is just such a solution for all, and it can begin in the early grades rather than waiting until high school. And for students of color, there is a cycle that needs to be broken where the early warning signs (lack of early literacy, grade retention, absenteeism, school disengagement, etc.) are the very things that some of their schools struggle with to create success for all students (APA, 2010). For a comprehensive list of the early warning signs of student disengagement to use in order to build supports for these students see items 7–10 in the appendix.

In response to this problem, Michigan schools are encouraged to enlist ten to fifteen African American male students with the largest needs in terms of dropout ABCs (attendance, behavior, and course proficiency) into a supportive school program called the Superintendent's Dropout Challenge, or just Dropout Challenge (Doll, 2014). This program works by having an adult advocate (a teacher, paraprofessional, other staff, volunteer, district administrator, custodian, and so forth) work regularly with each student to help in the targeted area(s) of improvement. Though this is an optional program for schools across the state, it is also required for a small percentage of schools where the students need help the most. A total of 15 percent of Michigan's schools (about five hundred) are identified for corrective actions because of persistent academic needs in them, and they are *required* to participate in the Dropout Challenge. There are two types of schools under correction: Focus Schools, which have large achievement gaps among students, and Priority Schools with low student achievement.

The requirement for Focus and Priority Schools to participate in the Dropout Challenge was instituted in the fall of 2012, and research has been conducted in both of the ensuing school years on general trends among students. For instance, among the 6,800 students who were supported by the Dropout Challenge in 2012–13, they were mainly struggling with poor *Course proficiency/Grades* (72 percent of the students), *Family-related* issues (58 percent) and *Lack of classroom participation* (50 percent). Also, in Priority Schools, where students were struggling more with lower assessments, there were peaks in *Attendance-related* problems (61 percent) and also *Repetitive behavior referrals* (60 percent). Surprisingly, in Focus Schools, where there was a very large gap between highest-performing and lowest-performing learners, these concerns were abated dramatically with *Attendance-related* problems at only 31 percent and *Repetitive behavior referrals* even lower at 27 percent. As insightful as this initial research was, an analysis was not conducted that could specifically be beneficial to school leaders and policy makers who were trying to help African American males. That created the inspiration for this research project.

Research Questions

From the start of the 2013–14 school year, it was understood that the research on the Dropout Challenge should be poised to assist school leaders and policy makers whose daily work is in promoting opportunities for African American males. After all, the state of Michigan has recognized that African American males are the lowest-achieving subgroup of any other ethnicity and gender combination (Michigan State Board of Education, 2012). As a result, three research questions were created to guide this project, as follows:

1. Do schools vary significantly in the percentages of African Americans enrolled?
2. Do schools also differ significantly in how students are supported to prevent eventual dropout?
3. Do schools differ in the types of struggles of their students, and if so, how can schools react proactively to support African American male students?

Methodology

In order to answer the three highly focused research questions, a way was needed to isolate schools where there was a high percentage of African American males and compare them with schools that were lower. Research in 2012–13 had shown that students supported by the Dropout Challenge were about 63 percent male and also 37 percent African American, which meant that in many schools, there might be a good chance to observe African American males as the chosen supported students. Still, however, it was possible that in schools where there were not as many African American students enrolled, the supported students might not even be African Americans at all.

As a result of these concerns, it was prudent to compare two subsets of the approximately five hundred Focus and Priority Schools: those with high percentages of African American students enrolled (75 percent or greater) and those with low percentages enrolled (25 percent or fewer). In just such a way, the former group might be a good test case to identify the challenges that supported students face, since they were most likely to be African American males. Thus, it would be possible to compare the issues of these students with supported students in schools that lacked African Americans, in some cases altogether. As a result, findings from this research could help us form guided understandings for what support African American males might need the most in dropout prevention as compared with the other students.

Settlement patterns primarily in urban centers like Detroit, Grand Rapids, and Flint allowed for significant numbers of schools to be included in the research

TABLE 1. Number and Types of Schools Where the Dropout Challenge Was Conducted

SCHOOLS WITH ABOVE 75% OF AFRICAN AMERICANS	SCHOOLS WITH BELOW 25% OF AFRICAN AMERICANS
Number = 76	Number = 321
74 Priority Schools (97.4%)	27 Priority Schools (8.4%)
2 Focus Schools (2.6%)	294 Focus Schools (91.6%)

sample: as a result, there were 76 schools with 75 percent or greater of African Americans enrolled and 321 schools with 25 percent or fewer African Americans. Table 1 shows that there was a combined total of 397 schools, which was 79 percent of the total number of about 500 schools under correction. As indicated in the table, a much higher level of Priority Schools could be found in communities where school enrollment was tipped toward African Americans (97 percent compared to 8 percent), while there was also an inverse relationship in the rate of Focus Schools (3 percent compared to 92 percent). As a confirmation that dropout prevention can take place at schools other than high schools, the majority of schools in the sample were middle schools (57.9 percent of the schools with above 75 percent of African Americans) or K–5 buildings (41.7 percent of schools with 25 percent or fewer African Americans).

As stated previously, a strong majority of the schools with higher rates of African Americans (86 percent) were located in urban areas, and no similar subset of schools were in rural areas. On the other hand, schools with relatively few African Americans were primarily rural or in small towns (43 percent) or suburban (33 percent) with the remaining share in urban areas. The breakdown of ethnicities in schools illuminates quite a lot about Michigan's settlement patterns, as depicted in table 2. Thus, a very strong majority of African Americans are in many of the seventy-six schools with higher rates of African Americans, such that only one other ethnicity exceeds a 3 percent threshold, and then only slightly. Conversely, schools with lower rates of African Americans are much more predominantly White, Hispanic, or Asian, or Multiracial.

In the fall of 2013, school principals were given a fourteen-question survey through surveymonkey.com (see appendix), which asked them questions about common struggles of the students who were supported in dropout prevention and about the structure of the school's support for those students. Because of the

TABLE 2. Average Percentages of Ethnicities of Students in Schools

AMERICAN INDIAN	ASIAN	BLACK	HAWAIIAN	WHITE	HISPANIC	MULTIRACIAL
Schools with above 75% of African Americans						
0.2%	0.6%	94.0%	0.1%	3.1%	1.5%	0.5%
Schools with below 25% of African Americans						
1.4%	4.8%	7.6%	0.1%	75.7%	6.9%	3.4%
Average in All Schools						
1.2%	4.0%	24.1%	0.1%	61.9%	5.9%	2.9%

comprehensive work of the large group of stakeholders that support Michigan's schools (independent school districts and district consultants, higher education consultants, and so forth), a 99 percent response rate was achieved on this survey, as could be compared with 99 percent response rates that were also attained the previous year.

Results

When did schools join the dropout challenge? Schools primarily joined the Dropout Challenge at the start of the previous two school years. This result supports the idea that at the designated time, school leaders recognized and complied with the requirement of this schoolwide early warning signs intervention.

How did schools choose their students? Generally speaking, and among both school types, there were significant percentages of schools that had either recently joined the Dropout Challenge or who were continuing in their second year and only needed to add a small number of students (less than 10).

What grade levels were represented among the 6,225 supported students in the 2013–14 school year? Though a bell-shaped curve is often indicative of a balance being reached in research findings, the higher concentration of middle schools in this research sample is mainly responsible for the higher number of students at these grade levels. As a note, Michigan's school enrollment is nearly identically spread through each grade level statewide (Michigan Department of Education, 2013).

FIGURE 1. When Schools Joined the Dropout Challenge

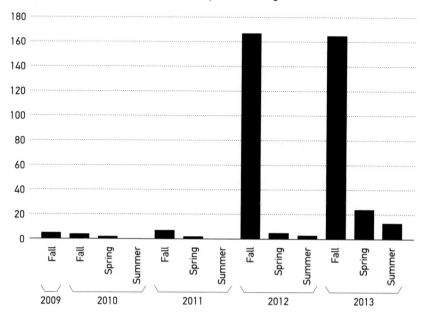

FIGURE 2. The Selection of Students

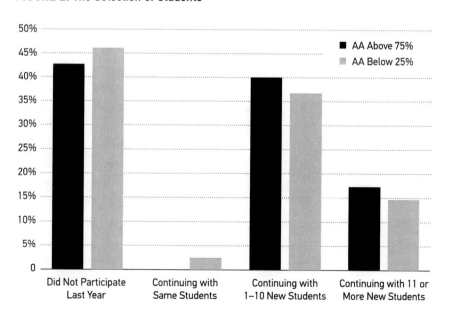

Who were the adult advocates for these students? There are many types of adults working with supported students; that said, African American males may be more likely to be supported by school counselors (16 percent), community members (13 percent), assistant principals (11 percent), or graduation coaches (3 percent), which each highlight a role delegated by principals. Also, these students might be less likely to be served by principals and teachers of record or not of record than their peers in schools with lower rates of African American students. One message from these statistics is that principals and teachers of African American students were focusing on other areas, such as academics or possibly discipline, rather than working directly with these students in dropout prevention. Quite possibly, as well, counselors, graduation coaches, and assistant principals were the best in-school staff to work in dropout prevention, while community members were also lending a hand.

Who were the 256 other adult advocates? Survey responses included an open-ended category for "Other" types of adult advocates. It was quite interesting that over 17 percent of the adults who supported students in either school setting listed the choice "Other" instead of the other eight categories. Open-ended responses for "Other" included janitors, classroom assistants, coaches, deans, paraprofessionals, parent assistants, and so forth, reflecting the resiliency of schools to rise to the challenge of supporting their students in any way possible.

Who are the dropout challenge monitors? Previous research had shown that students in Priority Schools were much less likely to have the principal be the person in charge of the Dropout Challenge, at 39 percent compared with 83 percent in Focus Schools (Doll & Bowerman, 2013). By looking at schools with high and low percentages of African Americans, these findings were confirmed, such that schools with high percentages of African Americans (mostly Priority Schools) balanced their work of managing the Dropout Challenge among many staff members so that the responsibility was shared.

What did the students struggle with? Another way of looking at a challenge is that it is a skill being developed. So, by investigating challenges of supported students in dropout prevention, we can catch a glimpse of the skills that schools are nurturing in them. There were four types of struggles that students faced as organized in the survey in questions 7–10. The four areas were Lifestyle Risk Factors, Academic

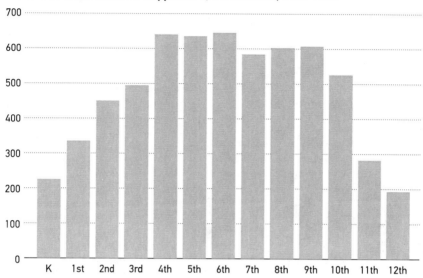

FIGURE 3. Grade Levels of Supported 6,225 Students, 2013–2014

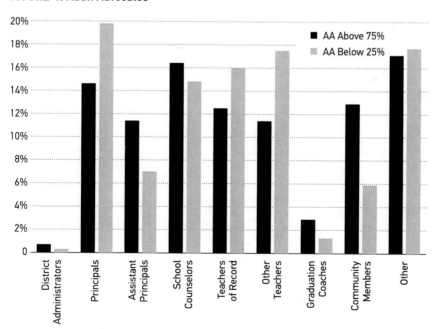

FIGURE 4. Adult Advocates

FIGURE 5. Dropout Challenge Monitors

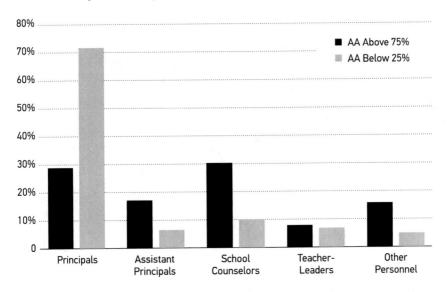

Disengagement/Frustration Risk Factors, Student Risk Factors, and School Risk Factors.

Each of the four groups of early warning signs were rated by principals in considering their supported students as a group. In that way, schools with high percentages of African Americans exhibited a high likelihood that the students being evaluated as a group were, in fact, African American males. On the other hand, schools with lower percentages of African Americans had less of a chance of this occurring. Each risk area was rated 1–5 on a scale from minor to severe, and the top two rankings (4 and 5) were collapsed to show when a risk area was significantly problematic for students.

More, in schools with fewer African Americans, only *Grades* and *Family-Related concerns* both ranked as high as 79%, which was higher than all other factors in questions 7–10.

■ **LIFESTYLE RISK FACTORS.** African American male students were more likely to struggle with *Attendance-related* and *Family-related* issues than their peers in schools with fewer African Americans. As such, schools in these areas can significantly build supports in truancy and having rigorous, relevant instruction that would draw

FIGURE 6. Attendance, Family, and Work

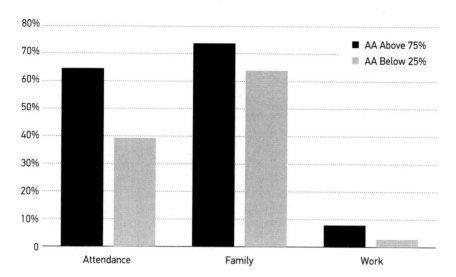

students to school. Also, added family supports and counseling for students can help acknowledge and mitigate challenges African American males may experience in families. The area of *Work-related* as a risk area was only evaluated by high schools and was considered minor by students of both school types.

■ **ACADEMIC DISENGAGEMENT/FRUSTRATION RISK FACTORS.** African American male students and non–African American students had as a primary struggle their success in academic coursework (*Course proficiency/Grades*), and this needs the most remediation at every school level. Also, *Lack of class participation* and *Lack of connections with classmates* were more of a struggle for African American males, which could be helped most by the dedicated work of dynamic, caring teachers, teacher leaders, and school administration/counselors. It should be noted that academic disengagement is a cumulative process, not a spontaneous event (Rumberger, 2011). As a result, targeted efforts by school staff (teachers, administrators, counselors) need to be further supported by all staff, community members, and volunteers to create a sense of trust within the school culture that can help build deeper engagement and the ability of the school to reach the needs of their students in consistent, replicable ways.

FIGURE 7. Grades, Participation, Peer Connections

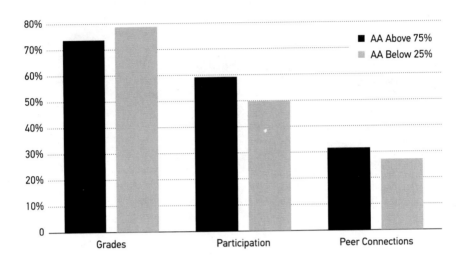

FIGURE 8. Behavior, Health, and Peer Pressure

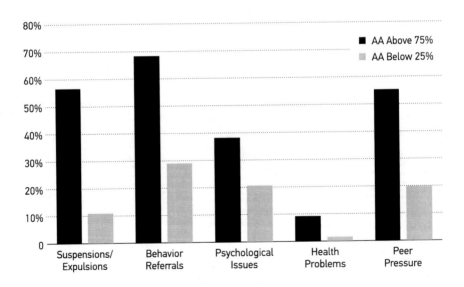

■ **STUDENT RISK FACTORS.** Of the five student risks that were evaluated, it was highly significant that these were considered minor (under 30 percent) in schools with low percentages of African Americans while they were much higher ranking (four of five above 30 percent; three above 50 percent) in schools with higher percentages of African Americans. From this, we can see that African American males given dropout prevention support struggled quite a lot with *Repetitive behavior referrals*, *Frequent suspensions/expulsions*, and *Peer pressure*. Data like this illuminates a highly charged school atmosphere where the attention and respect of students are at stake and alternatives to various forms of punishment need to be explored at every level. For students who have teachers from different cultures than their own, the challenge for students can be separating themselves from their peer group in order to learn. Such a challenge should not take place as a rule in schools where there are higher percentages of African Americans while not taking place nearly as much at schools with fewer African Americans. *Health problems* were a low-ranking concern, but still warrant intentional remediation so that this does not become more problematic in the future.

■ **SCHOOL RISK FACTORS.** Of school risk factors, principals ranked these at low rates, which hinted that they rated their work as effective for students. In order for that hope to be a consistent reality for African American males, schools should continually evaluate their effectiveness with students: in classes, in their counseling programs, and in the cultural relevancy of staff.

What were the top early warning risk factors (the top five)? Overall, as shown in table 3, *Grades* were the main concern for students in both school settings. There was not a primary difference between African American males and others, but rather the presence of commonalities. Despite some similarities, African American males supported in dropout prevention still tended to struggle more with *Repeated referrals, Attendance problems, Classroom participation,* and *Suspensions and expulsions*, with each of these high-risk areas occurring at rates over 50 percent. More, in schools with fewer African Americans, only *Grades* and *Family-related issues* ranked above 50%. An insight for school leaders/staff is that the work on both policies and practices can help unbundle these areas so they are not intertwined, to prevent referrals from *likely leading* to suspensions and expulsions, or low attendance from *often being followed* by low participation in class when students are present. Not every problem can be solved by one solution, but

FIGURE 9. School Risk Factors

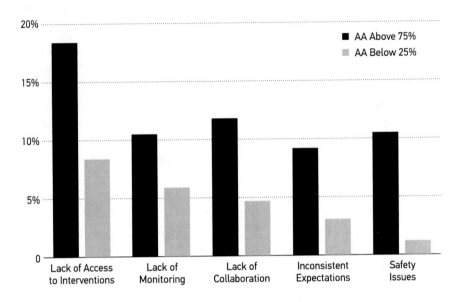

strategic work to prevent worst case scenarios can lead to significant progress and opportunities for all students.

What was the frequency of monitoring supported students' needs? Finally, schools of both types stated in one voice that they worked hard to provide weekly or monthly monitoring of students in the Dropout Challenge, confirming previous research in this area (Doll & Bowermann, 2013). Continued follow-up with students through adult advocates can give students access to relationships that also might fill voids in other areas of life. In so doing, a farmer's adage can be fulfilled, that *two* birds can be fed with *one* cob of corn.

Discussion

Collaboration is at the heart of success in organizations, and so in focusing this discussion I would like to highlight the collective nature of answers that we all (educators, practitioners, administrators, researchers, teachers, and students themselves) seek to educational problems so that they become opportunities.

TABLE 3. The Top Five Early Warning Risk Factors

#	SCHOOLS WITH ABOVE 75% OF AFRICAN AMERICANS	SCHOOLS WITH BELOW 25% OF AFRICAN AMERICANS
1	Grades/Family-Related Issues (73.7%)	Grades (78.8%)
2	Repeated Referrals (68.4%)	Family-Related Issues (63.9%)
3	Attendance Problems (64.5%)	Classroom Participation (49.8%)
4	Classroom Participation (59.2%)	Attendance Problems (39.3%)
5	Suspensions and Expulsions (56.6%)	Repeated Referrals (29.0%)

FIGURE 10. Frequency of Monitoring Students

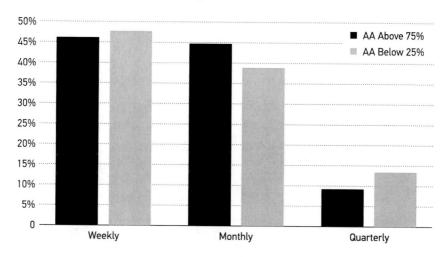

Thus, as we consider this research project that was extended to learning more about supports needed for African American males, it is sensible to return to the previous research questions and ascertain their solutions.

Research Questions Revisited
Do Schools Vary Significantly in the Percentages of African Americans Enrolled?

The answer was a resounding yes, that in seventy-six schools where there are high percentages of African Americans enrolled, students were in urban areas mostly enrolled in schools with state-identified low academic performance. Also, the 321 schools with low percentages of African Americans were primarily suburban or rural and had achievement gaps between students as their primary challenge.

Settlement patterns throughout Michigan harken back to an industrial era of cars and big business that we are slowly returning to. Decentralizing districts and creating county districts is one idea that could help balance funding mechanisms in areas where there is a greater imbalance between poverty and resources. At the same time, no educator or state representative can allow systemic issues to impede the equal access to appropriate educational services for all students. Instead of trying to ignore or erase the history that has made this state what it is, it is incumbent on all of us as educators to find ways of fixing schools and extending opportunities to all students that will help right the equilibrium of economic opportunities statewide. One example is to use the positive behavior supports (PBS) model, also known as PBIS when considering the interventions in schools, to not only correctly identify students who need added supports, but to go one step further and make as a school rule that you find the strengths in the students you are trying to help (OSEP, 2014).

As the authors of *Strengths Based Leadership* contend, "effective leaders surround themselves with the right people and build on each person's strengths" (Rath & Conchie, 2008, p. 21). We can extend that to say that "effective school leaders," and even "effective students," are people who choose the right peers and then build each other's strengths. In my research, I have taken that one step further. I posit that it is not enough to provide years of support to these students in hopes of averting a desperate or hate-filled act. Instead, the schools with their effective PBS/PBIS system should continually assess and invest in the *strengths* of those who are supported so that the students themselves find the high road of success in their lives rather than the low road of failure and consequences coming from that failure.

Do Schools also Differ Significantly in How Students Are Supported to Prevent Eventual Dropout?

There were many areas where students from the two school types (low versus high percentages of African Americans) differed in either their receipt of services or the struggles that they encountered. While the goal of keeping students enrolled and successful in school may be common in schools of both types, the pathway that is followed in each building differs. With regard to African American males, it was more common that they were supported in their schools by adult advocates who were assistant principals, counselors, graduation coaches, or community members, and less by principals, teachers of record, or teachers who were not of record (i.e., without a teaching role over the student). That said, it may be important that highly tasked principals and teachers in these schools appreciate the supportive role taken by assistant principals, community members, and counselors. In addition, these schools can work to find ways to increase the supportive role of teachers in dropout prevention as well as principals in ways that the supportive role can be an additional alternative form of discipline (i.e., suspension or expulsion, where it Second, the dropout prevention programs for African American males were not as often monitored by principals, but instead by assistant principals, counselors, or "Other" participants like community members, paraprofessionals, or volunteers. In this way, it is critical to note that the organizational knowledge of dropout prevention in schools with higher percentages of African American males may not always be percolating up to the awareness of principals, which might in turn be a shortcoming for these schools in developing comprehensive systems to help African American males. Therefore, principals in these schools should make an extra effort to be an intermediary between supported students and their classroom teachers so that dropout prevention through early warning signs becomes a whole-school effort and resulting collection of success stories.

Lastly, there were several key areas where schools of both types did not differ significantly: the timing of their involvement in the intervention, how they chose their students, what grade levels were represented, and the frequency of monitoring them. In terms of timing, nearly all schools tended to join the Dropout Challenge either in fall 2012 or fall 2013, which was when they were named as Priority or Focus Schools. Also, over 80 percent of students in both school settings were either new altogether to the program (new group of 10–15 students) or were partly new to the program (1–10 students being added to the previous year's group). In both cases, schools needed to train numerous staff and volunteers in working with an expected group of new students, which required an adequate level of capacity. In terms of grade levels, students were distinctly spread across all grades, kindergarten through twelfth grade, with a slightly greater amount in the middle school years. Finally, students from schools of both types were monitored on at least a weekly or a monthly basis, which could provide time for interventions like check-in, check-out (a dropout prevention and behavior-nurturing technique where adult relationships are used to model growth through regular connection) to make a lasting impact (PBIS World, 2014).

Do Schools Differ in the Types of Struggles of Their Students, and If So, How Can Schools React Proactively to Help African American Male Students?

In comparing schools with high and low percentages of African Americans enrolled, and hence high and low rates of African American males respectively, there were several major areas of increase in the severity of student struggles, some minor areas of decrease, and certain areas which were not seen as risk areas at all but which might still warrant further concern.

Areas of increase should be understood to be risks that are perceived as a far greater concern in schools with high rates of African American males. The top area of increase was *Suspensions and expulsions*, which was reported at a 46% higher rank in schools with higher percentages of African Americans (56.6 percent compared with 10.9 percent). This fundamental concern raised by schools should be the strongest impetus for all of us (state, district, school, and student levels) to seek and explore intentional solutions as alternatives to suspensions and expulsions. This was the largest area of increase and warrants the fullest attention in resolving. The second highest was in the area of *Repeated referrals*, which had a 39 percent higher rank in schools with high percentages of African Americans (68.4 percent compared with 29.0 percent). This area, which was also the second highest ranking among all sixteen variables, is connected with suspensions and expulsions and points toward the need for streamlined school discipline policy that recognize student strengths rather than emphasize or widen the potential for a gulf between what a student expresses and what an adult feels. In other words, we need to find ways to acknowledge and nurture positive behaviors while not letting off-task behavior lead to chronic classroom suspension and the school-initiated disengagement of students.

Peer pressure was another area that saw a large increase for schools with higher percentages of African Americans; it had a 35 percent higher rank in these schools (55.3 percent compared with 19.9 percent) and highlighted the need for more ways that teachers of African American males should work as an intermediary and trusted associate/confidant so as to strengthen positive peer relationships and help build collaborative behaviors as well. Lastly, the area of *Attendance* had a fairly large difference between schools of both types, with a 25 percent higher rank in schools with higher percentages of African Americans (64.5 percent compared with 39.3 percent). One instrumental way that schools can supplement their current work in improving African American male attendance, as well as other early warning risk areas (in addition to family and counseling supports in schools), is through an intervention Dr. Ivory Toldson and Dr. Chance Lewis have put forth called Positive Phone Calls Home, where schools intentionally and regularly make phone calls (and other forms of communication) home for African American male students' families and guardians to provide encouragement and a foundation of constructive relationships with schools. In Michigan, this intervention is used with great success in an initiative called the African American Young Men of Promise Initiative that targets improving educational opportunities for African American males.

There were only a small number of areas of comparatively lower-ranking survey responses seen in schools with higher percentages of African Americans. In other words, the school leaders tended to report the struggles of students with greater voracity than schools where there were lower percentages of African Americans. As such, the only risk area reported at a lower rate was that of Grades, with a decreased rate of 5 percent (73.7 percent compared to 78.8 percent). Ironically, schools of both types had also reported grades as the highest ranking of all the early warning signs, so while even being a comparatively smaller problem in one school type it was perceived as the largest concern of both school types altogether. As we consider that African American males who may struggle with school completion evidence this primarily in grades, it may be useful for schools to explore alternative interventions such as Saturday school and summer school, where these are not already in place, so as to help increase the potential influence that grades can have while at the same time avoiding consequences that course failure can initiate. The only other observed decreases were seen in the area of the frequency with which adult advocates interacted with students. As such, African American males were reported to receive less monitoring on a weekly or quarterly basis, which in turn means that most monitoring was provided to them on a monthly basis. Applying this knowledge, schools in working with African American males should realize that risk areas for students may seem more vibrant at times, but that solutions might also need to be vibrant, poised correctly, and intentionally scaffolded to all students. Second, providing additional support to students once a month is not enough; it never is. Schools in working with African American males who struggle academically need to utilize the positive adult relationships offered in schools in order to develop and earn equity in the hearts of these important students. In so doing, and with a deliberate focus on the messages the students give, schools can adapt their practice and make whatever changes are necessary, so that the most possible educational successes can result.

The final difference between schools of both types was obscure, but bears mentioning. External factors of the student's experience are often things outside their immediate domain. School leaders were surveyed on five such areas: *Lack of access to specific interventions, Lack of monitoring of progress, Lack of collaboration by teachers, Inconsistent expectations by school staff,* and *Safety issues.* Surprisingly, each of these areas garnered somewhat low rates of responses (all under 20 percent). While schools with higher percentages of African Americans reported somewhat higher rates of responses (e.g., 18.4 percent compared to 8.4 percent for *Lack of access to specific interventions*), it was more likely that school leaders felt some form of threat in reporting these types of concerns in a survey to the state education agency. Another possibility is that schools may have these areas somewhat more under control when it comes to supporting students in dropout prevention. While it might be difficult to know for certain, it is worth mentioning that these areas are of critical importance, and thus schools of both types should make sure that issues of access, monitoring, collaboration, staff expectations, and safety are not things that can cause their students to become disengaged and later drop out of school.

Conclusion

This research has attempted to explain behaviors schools can nurture and support areas that have been seen as helpful in schools in Michigan for African American males. While this discussion has focused primarily on the struggles of African American males in completing their schooling years, it should be recognized that every educational system where African Americans are enrolled should perform its own equity analysis of how it works with these students. America has a history of slow but steady growth in civil rights, but oftentimes the only positive solutions have come through sacrifice and intentional action. With that in mind, the reader is encouraged to discern positive intentional and fruitful actions they can take within and beyond their realm of influence to promote the widespread, continued successes of African American males.

It's something that if we all engage in it together, we can look back and be thankful for the opportunity to be doing the right thing at the right time.

REFERENCES

APA (American Psychological Association). (2010). *Facing the school dropout dilemma.* Washington, DC: American Psychological Association.

Borden-Conyers, J. (2014). Student voice preliminary findings in 28 low-performing Michigan schools. Los Angeles: Quincy & Associates, Inc.

Bridgeland, J. M., Dilulio, J. J., & Morison, K. B. (2006). *The silent epidemic: Perspectives of high school dropouts*. Washington, DC: Civic Enterprises.

Doll, J. (2010). *Teachers' and administrators' perceptions of the antecedents of school dropout among English language learners at selected Texas schools* (Unpublished doctoral dissertation). Texas A&M University, College Station.

————. *The ten tenets of the Superintendent's Dropout Challenge for focus and priority schools.* Retrieved from http://www.michigan.gov.

Doll, J., & Bowerman, R. (2013). National Dropout Prevention Center 2013, Michigan Department of Education presentation. http://www.michigan.gov.

Ford, W. (2013). *Problem solver: Dr. Ivory A. Toldson*. Retrieved from http://diverseeducation. com/?emerging-scholar=problem-solver-dr-ivory-a-toldson.

MI School Data. (2014). *2013 cohort four-year, 2012 cohort five-year and 2011 six-year graduation and dropout Rates including subgroups.* Retrieved from http://www.michigan.gov.

Michigan Department of Education. (2012). *Michigan State Board of Education and Michigan Department of Education goal and reform priorities 2012–2013.* Lansing: Michigan Department of Education.

Michigan Department of Education. (2013). MDE fast facts 2013–2014. Lansing: Michigan Department of Education.

National Public Radio (2013). *Are there really more black men in prison than college?* Retrieved from http://www.npr.org.

NCES (National Center for Education Statistics). (2013). *Public school graduates and dropouts from the common core of data: School year 2009–10.* Washington, DC: U.S. Department of Education.

OSEP (Office of Special Education Programs, Technical Assistance Center). (2014). *What is school-wide PBIS?* Retrieved from http://www.pbis.org/school/default.aspx.

PBIS World. (2014). *Check in check out (CICO).* Retrieved from http://www.pbisworld.com/tier-2/check-in-check-out-cico/.

Rath, T., & Conchie, B. (2008). *Strengths based leadership: Great leaders, teams, and why people follow.* New York: Gallup Press.

Rich, M. (2014). Obama to report widening of initiative for Black and Latino boys. *New York Times.*

Rumberger, R. W. (2011). *Dropping out: Why students drop out of high school and what can be done about it.* Cambridge, MA: Harvard University Press.

DROPOUT SURVEY

1. Are you a Priority School or Focus School? ☐ PRIORITY SCHOOL   ☐ FOCUS SCHOOL

2. Select your school: [LIST]

3. When did your school first join the Superintendent's Dropout Challenge?

☐ FALL 2009	☐ FALL 2010	☐ FALL 2011	☐ FALL 2012	☐ FALL 2013
☐ SPRING 2010	☐ SPRING 2011	☐ SPRING 2012	☐ SPRING 2013	☐ SPRING 2014
☐ SUMMER 2010	☐ SUMMER 2011	☐ SUMMER 2012	☐ SUMMER 2013	

4. Is your school supporting all of the same students you supported in the Superintendent's Dropout Challenge last year?

☐ DID NOT PARTICIPATE LAST YEAR

☐ PARTICIPATED LAST YEAR, AND ARE SUPPORTING ONLY THE SAME STUDENTS THIS YEAR

☐ PARTICIPATED LAST YEAR, AND ADDED 1–10 NEW STUDENTS THIS YEAR

☐ PARTICIPATED LAST YEAR, AND ADDED 11 OR MORE NEW STUDENTS THIS YEAR

5. Please describe the 10–15 (or more) students for your school that you have chosen for this school year.

☐ KINDERGARTEN	☐ GRADE 1	☐ GRADE 2	☐ GRADE 3	☐ GRADE 4	☐ GRADE 5
☐ GRADE 6	☐ GRADE 7	☐ GRADE 8	☐ GRADE 9	☐ GRADE 10	☐ GRADE 11
☐ GRADE 12	TOTAL (AT LEAST 10–15): _____				

6. You are required to have a Caring Adult for each of the selected students in the Superintendent's Dropout Challenge to be responsible to monitor/provide support for them. Describe this person/persons. Select all that apply.

☐ DISTRICT ADMINISTRATOR   ☐ PRINCIPAL   ☐ ASST. PRINCIPAL(S)

☐ SCHOOL COUNSELOR(S)

☐ TEACHER(S) WHO IS TEACHER-OF-RECORD FOR SUPPORTED STUDENTS

☐ TEACHER(S) WHO IS NOT TEACHER-OF-RECORD

☐ GRAD COACH

☐ COMMUNITY MEMBER/MENTOR

☐ OTHER CARING ADULT(S) NOT PREVIOUSLY IDENTIFIED, PLEASE SPECIFY: _____

(#7–#10) Relating only to the students selected this year for the Superintendent's Dropout Challenge, on a scale of 1–5 (with 1 being minor and 5 being severe), rate each of the following overall risk factors on your campus.

	MINOR				**SEVERE**
7. Lifestyle Risk Factors	**1**	**2**	**3**	**4**	**5**
ATTENDANCE-RELATED	—	—	—	—	—
FAMILY-RELATED	—	—	—	—	—
WORK-RELATED (HS ONLY)	—	—	—	—	—

8. Academic Disengagement/Frustration Risk Factors

COURSE PROFICIENCY/GRADES	—	—	—	—	—
LACK OF CLASSROOM PARTICIPATION	—	—	—	—	—
LACK OF CONNECTIONS WITH CLASSMATES	—	—	—	—	—

9. Student Risk Factors

FREQUENT SUSPENSIONS/EXPULSIONS	—	—	—	—	—
REPETITIVE BEHAVIOR REFERRALS	—	—	—	—	—
PSYCHOLOGICAL ISSUES	—	—	—	—	—
HEALTH PROBLEMS	—	—	—	—	—
PEER PRESSURE LEADING TO POOR DECISIONS	—	—	—	—	—

10. School Risk Factors

LACK OF ACCESS TO SPECIFIC INTERVENTIONS	—	—	—	—	—
LACK OF MONITORING OF PROGRESS	—	—	—	—	—
LACK OF COLLABORATION BY TEACHERS	—	—	—	—	—
INCONSISTENT EXPECTATIONS BY SCHOOL STAFF	—	—	—	—	—
SAFETY ISSUES	—	—	—	—	—

11. Relating only to the students selected for the Superintendent's Dropout Challenge, what are the top two early warning risk factors? (List includes all choices from #7–#10.)

TOP RISK FACTOR: _____   SECOND-HIGHEST RISK FACTOR: _____

12. Are there additional factor(s) that apply to your selected students that are NOT listed above in questions 7–10?

☐ YES   ☐ NO

IF YES, PLEASE SPECIFY: _____

13. You are required to have one person who monitors your school's participation in the Superintendent's Dropout Challenge. Describe this person:

☐ PRINCIPAL   ☐ ASST. PRINCIPAL   ☐ SCHOOL COUNSELOR   ☐ TEACHER-LEADER

☐ OTHER PARAPROFESSIONAL/PERSONNEL

14. State how often you will directly meet with selected students as you participate in the Superintendent's Dropout Challenge?

☐ WEEKLY   ☐ MONTHLY   ☐ QUARTERLY

IF DESIRED, PLEASE DESCRIBE HOW YOU WILL SUPPORT THESE STUDENTS: _____

_____

Smartphones

A Mobile Platform for Greater Learning, Equity, and Access

Kevin K. Green, Robert L. Green, and Theodore S. Ransaw

The color of the skin is in no way connected with strength of the mind or intellectual powers.

—Benjamin Banneker

In 1999 African American students from Inglewood, California, represented by the American Civil Liberties Union (ACLU) filed a lawsuit against the state of California to allow students equal access to advanced placement (AP) classes. Known as the *Daniel v. California* case, this trial challenged America to rethink its policies of college access and education equity. This was all because students from Inglewood High School were unable to enroll in math and science AP courses. Why? Because Inglewood High School did not offer AP courses in math or science. However, other high schools in neighboring but more affluent neighborhoods, such as Beverly Hills High School and Arcadia High School, not only offered AP classes in math and science, they also offered classes on computer programming and physics. The *Daniel v. California* case is just one example of how schooling is not the same for all students in America (Oakes, Joseph, & Muir, 2004).

In 2014, the Grand Rapids Public Schools (GRPS) retained Robert L. Green & Associates as consultants to examine the underrepresentation of African American students in college and career preparatory (CCP) courses[1] and make recommendations on what measures the district can take to address equal access disparities and help increase African American student enrollment in the following:

- CCP courses offered by the district, including the district's International Baccalaureate (IB) program at City Middle/High School, AP courses, dual enrollment courses, Centers of Innovation, and high school honors courses;
- Three specialty sixth-grade feeder schools (i.e., Zoo, Blandford, and the Center for Economicology);
- Foundation courses at the elementary, middle school, and high school levels, that is, those courses that are necessary for enrollment in CCP of specialty courses/programs/schools.

Furthermore, the consultant agreed to

- Examine and make recommendations to address the root cause(s) of any disparity in enrollment of African Americans in CCP courses, feeder schools, and foundation courses;
- Assess the degree and extent of what the district has done to address these disparities;
- Suggest recommendations that are outlined in Action Step II of the OCR Resolution Agreement in a written final report and assist the district, as requested, in alleviating these disparities.

Fortunately, the GRPS, under the leadership of Superintendent Teresa Neal and her leadership team, is working successfully to overcome and address past racial inequities in the GRPS system. The past inequities, discussed in their report, put African American students at an academic disadvantage that manifested itself in many areas. Most importantly, as a result of these past inequities and low expectations in predominantly African American schools, African American students were underrepresented in rigorous CCP courses, programs, and schools.

The Green Team consultants reviewed and assessed the root causes of past racial discrimination and its current impact on African American student achievement and analyzed district efforts to address low African American student enrollment in rigorous academic programs. The consultants also made recommendations

designed to enhance district efforts to increase African American student enrollment in AP classes and other competitive courses, programs, and schools.

Nationally, the reality of unequal schooling is especially true if you are a
minority student or if you live in a low-income neighborhood and are interested in
getting into college. Science, technology, engineering, and mathematics (STEM)–
focused classes geared toward college-seeking individuals are frequently not an
option for low-income or minority students.

African American males are underrepresented in STEM for many reasons,
including lack of K–12 exposure to STEM and also low academic expectations based
on stereotypes and media-influenced misperceptions of who should be scientists
(QEM, 2010). In fact, at least one study asserts that as the population of minority
students in a school increases the number of AP courses decreases (Oakes et al.,
2000). So what we are seeing is not just an economic digital divide for minority
students who live in disadvantaged neighborhoods, but opportunity gaps related
to access and adoption of technology for minorities. In other words, opportunity
gaps are related to digital gaps. The only way to change the balance of power in
educational opportunity gaps is to create learning environments where students
can help themselves on their terms.

High Expectations: A Force Multiplier in Student Achievement

Empowering students to be self-learners is akin to Paulo Freire's (1970) concept that
teachers should be more than depositors of information but facilitators of learning.
Freire (1970) begs education to be viewed as an interrelated relationship between
student, school and society. For Freire, education centers on integrating the younger
generation with present ways of doing things to achieve freedom. Green (2014) says,
expectations, the standards or the bar we set for others, are a factor in effort and
in outcomes. Teachers with high expectations will seek to have students achieve
those standards. Students will make an effort to meet those standards if they have
high expectations. Conversely, low expectations discourage effort and achievement,
while effective teachers hold high expectations for student success. The nation's
leading experts on education recognize the connection between teacher quality
and academic achievement. Learning through digital media such as smartphones
allows the student to be an active participant and the teacher to be a facilitator in
the education process. This type of pedagogy moves away from teachers merely

FIGURE 1. Economic and Internet Access Factors Are Adversely Impacting Achievement

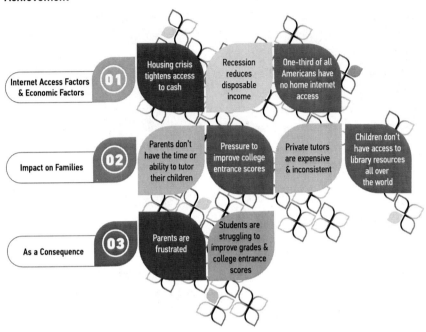

01 Internet Access Factors & Economic Factors
- Housing crisis tightens access to cash
- Recession reduces disposable income
- One-third of all Americans have no home internet access

02 Impact on Families
- Parents don't have the time or ability to tutor their children
- Pressure to improve college entrance scores
- Private tutors are expensive & inconsistent
- Children don't have access to library resources all over the world

03 As a Consequence
- Parents are frustrated
- Students are struggling to improve grades & college entrance scores

using students to recite what they have learned, but instead encourages students to be active participants in their education. Mobile devices such as smartphones can change the educational outcomes of economically disadvantaged students, particularly young Black males, by enhancing classroom environments where teachers make deposits of learning and students withdraw their engagement. In other words, using digital devices such as smartphones is a cool idea since it contains the potential of being an educational tool that will be more engaging, and most of all fun to use. Wilkins (2008) confirms that cool, put simply, intersects race, class, and gender.

Barriers to Learning

Students today have more after-school obligations—sports and clubs, jobs and other activities—than ever before. It is much more difficult for today's students to connect with their teachers after school for homework help. When they finally get home and are ready to do their math or science homework, they have no one to turn to for assistance. These students need supplemental educational support (e.g., tutoring), but parents have neither the time nor the ability to assist and private quality tutors are expensive. Additionally, because of staff cutbacks in many school districts, teachers often have larger classrooms and may not always have the time to provide assistance to their students that need additional attention during the day or after school. Moreover, some students cannot attend after-school sessions because their parents or guardians must provide transportation.

Private tutoring is one way to address barriers to after-school instruction, but in general, and especially as a result of the recession, few families can afford private tutors. Students could get remedial instruction via the Internet and software programs; however, many parents in communities with underperforming schools cannot afford home computers (Zickuhr & Smith, 2013). These impediments are summed up in figure 1.

The Negative Impacts of Federal Mandates on Today's School Districts

In addition to the barriers mentioned above, many financially strapped school districts are forced to rely on teachers who are not certified to teach math or science. Often, financially challenged school districts also have more underperforming schools (Green, White, & Green, 2012). Under the No Child Left Behind (NCLB) Act of 2001, a U.S. act of Congress concerning the education of children in public schools, students at those schools are eligible for tutoring, and much of that supplemental education is available online. But, again, students in homes without a computer cannot take advantage of those services, and they do not have online access to library resources around the world. Furthermore, the National Assessment of Educational Progress (NAEP) scores are low (NAEP, 2014). The NAEP, also known as "the nation's report card," is a periodic assessment of student progress conducted in the United States by the National Center for Education Statistics, a division of the U.S. Department of Education. Performance data has been conducted using a representative sample of fourth- and eighth-grade students in reading and mathematics for the past several decades, which allows for longitudinal comparisons of achievement gaps by racial/ethnic group and gender.

The Achievement Gap: Why It Matters

In grade 4 math, figure 2 and table 1 reveal that the average scale score among Black and Hispanic public school students (both males and females) increased between 2000 and 2013, but Black-White and Hispanic-White performance gaps closed only slightly since White students both made gains and started at higher performance levels.

In grade 8 math, figure 3 and table 2 show that the average scale score among Black and Hispanic public school students (both males and females) made substantial gains between 2000 and 2013 that were nearly twice those of White students, but achievement gaps again remained large due to higher starting points for Whites.

Gains in NAEP fourth-grade reading scores among all student subgroups were considerably smaller than in math (see figure 4 and table 3), with Black and Hispanic students' growth again outpacing that of Whites. Both the Black-White and Hispanic-White gaps remained in the twenty-five to twenty-six point range.

However, in grade 8 reading scores (see figure 5 and table 4), only Hispanic (both male and female) students had the largest gains with nearly twice those of both Black and White students, while Black and White students (both male and female) had almost similar gains (i.e., six point increase for Blacks and five point increase for Whites). Still, the achievement gap persists and currently is in the nineteen to twenty-six point range, due to White students starting at higher performance levels.

Achievement Implications: Predictor of High School and College Completion

The implications of educational attainment are significant, since it is a predictor of high school and college completion (Black-White and Hispanic-White gaps remain), as shown in table 5 and table 6, and also a predictor of somebody's earnings according to degree type (U.S. Census, 2012a) as shown in table 7.

Achievement Implications: Predictor of Yearly Earnings

The 2009 data from the Current Population Survey (U.S. Census, 2012b) summarized below in Table 7 on earnings by educational attainment level and subgroup, reveal that those who fail to earn a high school diploma can expect to earn, on average, approximately $20,000 annually (and even less for Black and Hispanic workers).

FIGURE 2. NAEP National Public Grade 4 Math Scale Score by Subgroup, Selected Years 2000–2013

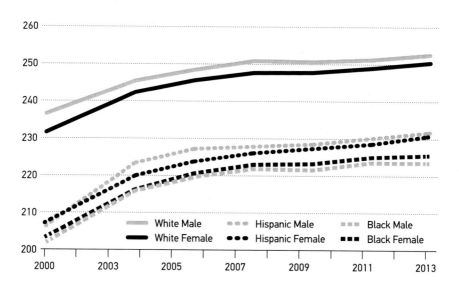

TABLE 1. Grade 4 NAEP Math Scale Scores by Subgroup, Selected Years 2000–2013

	2000	2003	2005	2007	2009	2011	2013	CHANGE
White Male	236	244	247	249	249	250	251	+15
White Female	231	241	244	246	246	248	249	+18
Hispanic Male	207	223	227	228	228	230	231	+24
Hispanic Female	208	220	223	226	226	228	230	+22
Black Male	202	216	219	221	221	223	223	+21
Black Female	204	216	220	223	223	225	225	+21

FIGURE 3. NAEP National Public Grade 8 Math Scale Score by Subgroup, Selected Years 2000–2013

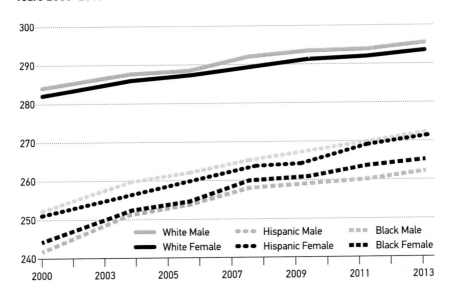

TABLE 2. Grade 8 NAEP Math Scale Scores by Subgroup, Selected Years 2000–2013

	2000	2003	2005	2007	2009	2011	2013	CHANGE
White Male	284	287	288	292	293	293	295	+11
White Female	282	286	287	289	291	292	293	+11
Hispanic Male	252	260	262	265	267	270	272	+20
Hispanic Female	251	257	260	264	264	269	271	+20
Black Male	242	251	254	258	259	260	262	+20
Black Female	244	252	255	260	261	264	265	+21

FIGURE 4. NAEP National Public Grade 4 Reading Scale Score by Subgroup, Selected Years 2002–2013

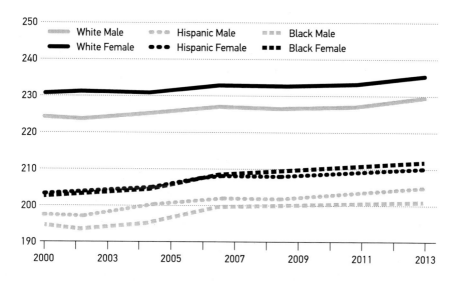

TABLE 3. Grade 4 NAEP Reading Scale Scores by Subgroup, Selected Years 2002–2013

	2000	2003	2005	2007	2009	2011	2013	CHANGE
White Male	224	223	225	227	226	227	229	+5
White Female	231	231	231	233	232	233	235	+4
Hispanic Male	197	196	199	201	201	203	204	+7
Hispanic Female	202	203	204	207	207	208	210	+8
Black Male	193	192	194	199	199	200	200	+7
Black Female	202	202	204	207	209	210	211	+9

FIGURE 5. NAEP National Public Grade 8 Reading Scale Score by Subgroup, Selected Years 2000–2013

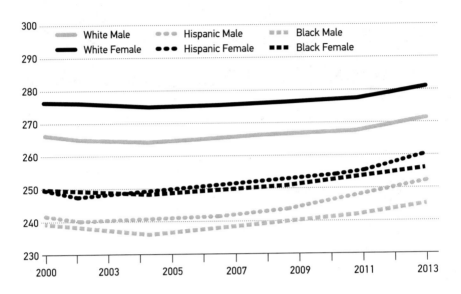

TABLE 4. Grade 8 NAEP Reading Scale Scores by Subgroup, Selected Years 2000–2013

	2000	2003	2005	2007	2009	2011	2013	CHANGE
White Male	266	265	264	265	267	267	271	+5
White Female	276	276	275	275	276	277	281	+5
Hispanic Male	241	240	241	241	243	248	252	+11
Hispanic Female	249	248	249	250	252	255	260	+11
Black Male	239	238	236	238	240	242	245	+6
Black Female	250	249	248	250	251	253	256	+6

TABLE 5. High School Completion Rates (Age 25 and Older) by Subgroup, Select Years

YEAR	ALL RACES			WHITE			BLACK			ASIAN			HISPANIC		
	TOTAL	M	F	TOTAL	M	F	TOTAL	M	F	TOTAL	M	F	TOTAL	M	F
2012	87%	87%	88%	88%	88%	88%	85%	84%	86%	89%	90%	88%	65%	64%	66%
2005	85%	85%	86%	86%	85%	86%	81%	81%	81%	88%	90%	85%	59%	58%	59%
2000	84%	84%	84%	85%	85%	85%	79%	79%	78%	NA	NA	NA	57%	57%	58%
1990	78%	78%	78%	79%	79%	79%	66%	66%	67%	NA	NA	NA	51%	50%	51%
1980	69%	69%	68%	71%	71%	70%	51%	51%	51%	NA	NA	NA	45%	46%	44%
1970	55%	55%	55%	57%	57%	58%	34%	32%	35%	NA	NA	NA	NA	NA	NA

TABLE 6. College Completion (Four Years) Rates (Age 25 and Older) by Subgroup, Select Years

YEAR	ALL RACES			WHITE			BLACK			ASIAN			HISPANIC		
	TOTAL	M	F	TOTAL	M	F	TOTAL	M	F	TOTAL	M	F	TOTAL	M	F
2012	31%	31%	31%	31%	31%	31%	21%	19%	23%	51%	54%	49%	15%	13%	16%
2005	28%	29%	27%	28%	29%	27%	18%	16%	19%	50%	54%	47%	12%	12%	12%
2000	26%	28%	24%	26%	29%	24%	17%	16%	17%	NA	NA	NA	11%	11%	11%
1990	21%	24%	18%	22%	25%	19%	11%	12%	11%	NA	NA	NA	9%	10%	9%
1980	17%	21%	14%	18%	22%	14%	8%	8%	8%	NA	NA	NA	8%	10%	6%
1970	11%	14%	8%	12%	15%	9%	5%	5%	4%	NA	NA	NA	NA	NA	NA

Income earned by those without a high school diploma is approximately two-thirds of what will be earned by those with a high school diploma, one-third that of someone who earns a bachelor's degree, one-fourth of someone with a master's degree, and one-fifth of someone with a PhD. All of these additional barriers to learning in school districts today are summarized in figure 6.

STEM, STEAM, and STREAM: Adding Reading, Writing, and the Arts

Robert and Michele Root-Bernstein, the coauthors of *Sparks of Genius: The 13 Thinking Tools of the World's Most Creative People* and *Honey, Mud, Sparks of Maggots and Other Medical Marvels*, discussed in a March 2011 National Writing Project article the importance of including reading and writing, along with the arts, in training young students to become innovative and successful scientists. They discuss the movement to modify the STEM acronym (i.e., science, technology, engineering, and mathematics) into the STEAM acronym by adding the arts, and even further modification to become STREAM by adding reading and writing. They note that science educators realize that STEM professionals have benefitted from the arts and crafts visual thinking—for example, recognizing and forming patterns, modeling, and manipulating skills gained using pens and brushes. Next, they then cite that the National Science Foundation and the National Endowment for the Arts have begun formal meetings between the agencies to figure out how to fund research in the importance of teaching at the intersections of science and the arts, so that STEAM may condense to STREAM. Below is an excerpt from their NWP article:

> Writing, like any other art, teaches the entire range of "tools for thinking" that are required to be creative in any discipline. To be a lucid writer, one must observe acutely; abstract out the key information; recognize and create patterns; use analogies and metaphors to model in words some reality that takes place in another dimension; translate sensations, feelings, and hunches into clearly communicable forms; and combine all this sensual information into words that create not only understanding but also delight, remorse, anger, desire, or any other human emotion that will drive understanding into action.
>
> Think about it: what we've just described is what a scientist or mathematician does too.

TABLE 7. 2009 Earnings (in dollars) by Educational Attainment Level, Selected Subgroups

	NOT A HIGH SCHOOL GRADUATE	HIGH SCHOOL GRADUATE ONLY	SOME COLLEGE, NO DEGREE	ASSOCIATES	BACHELORS	MASTER'S	PROFESSIONAL	DOCTORATE
				MEAN EARNINGS BY LEVEL OF HIGHEST DEGREE (DOLLARS)				
ALL	20,241	30,627	32,295	39,771	56,665	73,738	127,803	103,054
Male	23,036	35,468	39,204	47,572	69,479	90,964	150,310	114,347
Female	15,514	24,304	25,340	33,432	43,589	58,534	89,897	83,708
WHITE	20,457	31,429	33,119	40,632	57,762	73,771	127,942	104,533
Male	23,353	36,418	40,352	48,521	71,286	91,776	149,149	115,497
Female	15,187	24,615	25,537	33,996	43,309	58,036	89,526	85,682
BLACK	18,936	26,970	29,129	33,734	47,799	60,067	102,328	82,510
Male	21,828	30,723	33,969	41,142	55,655	68,890	NA	NA
Female	15,644	22,964	25,433	29,464	42,587	54,523	NA	NA
HISPANIC	19,816	25,998	29,836	33,783	49,017	71,322	79,228	88,435
Male	21,588	28,908	35,089	38,768	58,570	80,737	NA	89,956
Female	16,170	21,473	24,281	29,785	39,566	61,843	NA	NA

FIGURE 6. American Schools and Federal Mandates Are Impacting School Districts

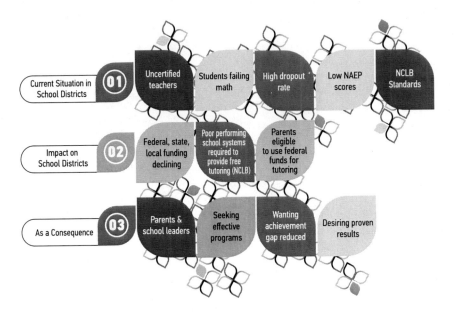

Furthermore, the authors discuss the importance of mastering one's own language, such as the ability to parse and manipulate it, in order to master the use of a STEM language—for example, Algebra 1 with all of its associated symbols and terminology. In the *Journal of Science* (Woodford, 1967; Miyake et al., 2010), these articles concluded that mastery of the English language is a prerequisite and an indicator in determining scientific success in STEM careers and academic performance in STEM courses. Additionally, in Kevin Green's (2009) book chapter entitled "Best Practices on How Teachers Can Instill Confidences and Competence in Math Students," he reinforces the importance of mastery of STEM language by having his math students create a glossary in the following excerpt:

> Another study technique is to have students create a glossary. I discovered through my years of teaching that if students don't understand the language of math, such as knowing certain terms and definitions, this knowledge gap affected their learning the lesson plan for the day. What I saw occurring was that if they did not know a certain term or definition being used, their mind would tend to get filled up with

such questions as "What does that word mean? What is he talking about?" His English has been transformed to some unknown tongue. As I shift from defining a term, I move on to the concept, and then a brief explanation and application of the concept. But, the student who had not taken the time to review previously taught terms and definitions are mentally caught in the first phase of not understanding the language. (Green, K., 2009, p. 196)

Lastly, the authors Root-Bernstein and Root-Bernstein (2011) conducted large statistical studies on the hobbies and avocations of the average scientist, from Nobel laureates to members of the U.S. National Academy of Sciences and the British Royal Society, and discovered that Nobel laureates and the members of these prestigious academies were at least twenty times and in some cases up to a hundred times as likely to have a writing avocation as the average scientist. The authors conclude that turning STEM into STEAM will empower the sciences, but adding reading and writing skills will create the STREAM from which STEAM can be produced!

The remainder of this chapter will examine new trends and directions of how smartphones support STEM, STEAM, and STREAM. We start with a brief overview of various learning barriers students may have in using technology in schooling that may be solved with mobile devices, and then cover technology and how technology can be used within and outside the classroom to increase academic achievement, particularly for African American students.

Project-Based Learning Incorporates STEM to Improve Academic Achievement

By integrating project-based learning (PBL), real-world internship experiences, and high expectations, a Cleveland, Ohio, high school is building a model of achievement in STEM. The Metropolitan Cleveland Consortium (MC2)—or MC2 STEM—was created in 2008 through a public-private partnership designed to pro-vide an integrated curriculum informed by real-world experiences. It is part of the Cleveland Metropolitan School District, one of the most economically challenged school districts in the nation, where the average high school graduation rate was just 60 percent in 2011. On the other hand, since the MC2 STEM opened, nearly 100 percent of students have graduated, and 84 percent of the graduates have enrolled in college. The keys to success at the school are an interdisciplinary PBL model, internships, and high expectations backed by substantial teaching and tutoring support. High expectations are embedded in the school's core principles, and "Master your own path" is an MC2 STEM credo. Students attend classes on the school campus and at sites located at technology companies and universities in the area. PBL students built a new audio system for a performance at the Cleveland-based Rock n' Roll Hall of Fame. Also, students sometimes get instruction from researchers at the NASA Glenn Center and were offered internship opportunities.

Online Culture and Learning, Technology, and STEM Education

The standards or the expectation that we set for others can be a major factor in effort and in outcomes. If teachers have high expectations for their students, students will strive to meet those standards, and conversely, low expectations have the negative outcome of discouraging effort and low achievement. Research on student achievement and classroom standards has identified that teachers or administrators with low expectations of their students advance fewer students of color into advanced or STEM courses and that students from poor communities are disproportionately steered into special education classes or schools. The list below highlights some of the many ways K–12 educators can leverage the power of the Internet and STEM learning aids inside and outside the classroom, programs that—with the urging of teachers—students can also use at home for supplemental STEM instruction:

- Raspberry Pi is a credit-card-sized single-board computer developed with the intention of promoting the teaching of basic computer science in schools (www.raspberrypi.org). This capable, tiny computer could be used to create a low-cost, sophisticated tablet that can then be used for presentations, word processing, and watching videos. Most important, it can be used to teach students about computer hardware and computer programming.
- Online, interactive simulations for math and science education from ExploreLearning (www.explorelearning.com) are one of the novel ways of making STEM topics fun and easier to learn. The Texas Science Initiative conducted a meta-analysis of more than sixty research studies that focused on identifying technology-related teaching strategies. Here are some of their key findings on the use of ExploreLearning's Gizmos:

- Manipulation strategies enable students to experience science by becoming active learners who participate in building their own understanding.
- Technology-enhanced instruction, including simulations, enables students to manipulate variables and quickly see the results.
- Inquiry-based learning provides opportunities to analyze data and encourages deep understanding.
- Manipulation strategies, technology-enhanced instruction, and inquiry-based learning were associated with an average gain of eighteen to twenty-four percentile points in student achievement.

- The National Science Foundation has numerous programs in STEM education, including some for K–12 students, such as the ITEST Program that supports the Global Challenge Award ITEST Program. STEM programs have been implemented in some Arizona schools to help students develop higher cognitive skills, enabling them to inquire about and learn techniques used by professionals in fields related to science, technology, engineering, and math.

- Project Lead the Way (PLTW) is a leading provider of STEM education curricular programs to middle and high schools in the United States (www.pltw.org). The national nonprofit organization has over 5,200 programs in more than 4,700 schools in all fifty states. Programs include a high school engineering curriculum called Pathway to Engineering, a high school biomedical sciences program, and a middle school engineering and technology program called Gateway to Technology. PLTW provides the curriculum and the teacher professional development and ongoing support to create transformational programs in schools, districts, and communities. PLTW programs have been endorsed by President Barack Obama and U.S. Secretary of Education Arne Duncan as well as various state, national, and business leaders.

- The Girl Game Company (GGC) is an online resource designed to increase the interest, capacity, and motivation of middle school girls to pursue courses and careers in information technology (IT). The long-term goal is to increase diversity in the STEM workforce, with a focus on girls and Latinas, and the short-term goals include increasing IT fluency and increasing the appeal of educational pathways to IT careers. The participants design and build computer games and publish and receive feedback in a virtual community. The members of GGC have produced more than two hundred games, and the best ones have been posted in the virtual GGC clubhouse at www.whyville.net.

- The MIND Research Institute is a national nonprofit organization dedicated to research on learning and the brain and the application of this research to the development of K–12 math education programs. MIND (www.mindresearch.net) has developed a visual, online math-instruction education process that taps into the way we are "wired" to learn. MIND's education programs teach all children—regardless of socioeconomic or cultural background—how to think, reason, and create mathematically.
- Khan Academy's math videos on YouTube have become a very popular choice for K–12 students to mine for useful learning videos. The two sites, Khan Academy and YouTube, could also be useful to teachers as relevant tools for remediation or supplemental instruction. Khan Academy (www.khanacademy.org) has eclipsed MIT's OpenCourseWare (OCW) in terms of videos viewed and subscribers.
- Homeschoolmath.net provides a comprehensive list of math instruction websites.
- Here is an excellent compendium of best practice in K–12 STEM education programs: http://www.shrm.org/hrdisciplines/staffingmanagement/documents/compendium.pdf.

High Expectations for the Online Culture

When students come to school we ask them to turn off their smartphones, shut down their laptops, and tune in to learning. In short, we ask them to unplug. However, most students born close to or in the twenty-first century are digital natives fluent in the use of technology, and we as teachers are mostly digital immigrants—not automatically hard-wired and comfortable using technology. What could be achieved if we bridged the gaps between technology, teacher/student relationships, and learning? Today's student uses technology to learn in new ways we may not realize. Using technology in the classroom is natural to them, so why not let those students do so (Brown & Fox, 2013)?

The modern students, African American males included, have grown up in a culture where their phone is a computer that allows them to text, search the libraries of the world, and watch access websites that are informative and interactive.

Because of the technology built into smartphones, mobile devices are changing not only what students learn but how they learn (Kukulska-Hulme, 2009). Brown and Fox (2013) report that because of technology and the Internet, today's students' brains are functioning cognitively differently than previous generations'. Today's students are no longer reading strictly from left to right. In fact, twenty-first-century students typically ignore the entire right-hand side of the text on a computer. This is an artifact of the differing screen size between viewing content on a smartphone (e.g., two inches horizontally) versus a desktop computer (e.g., fifteen inches horizontally). And since how a student interacts with today's technology versus previous generations is drastically different, their experiences with how they think and their learning preferences will be different. Consequently, students often form emotional attachments to their electronic devices because of the amount of time they spend on them (Vincent, 2006). Since African American teen students are more likely to have a smartphone than White teens (Pew Research Center, 2010), and African Americans also feel disconnected to schooling (Ransaw, 2013), it is not unreasonable to have high expectations for the use of smartphones to bridge education gaps.

This news is so promising because effective teachers with high expectations design learning activities to be engaging and motivational (Green, R. L., 2009) and can learn to transform these same activities to online learning activities. Online learning and student engagement fit well with African American students who view computer learning in the classroom as a reward for exemplary behavior, and encouraging the use of digital learning can also be a strong motivator to complete assigned classwork (Judge, 2005). Teachers with high expectations also create affirming, structured, and comfortable learning environments (Green, R. L., 2009), which is perfectly suitable for online learning.

A sense of community is especially important to modern students because they turn to social media for learning (Mancilla, 2014). African American children in general prefer to work collectively and achieve well in groups (Boykin, 1983;Slavin, 1977; Slavin & Oickle, 1981). Working collectively in groups through using social media on mobile devices is a form of "culturally modeling" socially accepted learning styles among African Americans (Lee, 2000). Kyeong-Ju Seo (2013), asserts that technology is a great way to support learners, promote problem solving, and help build a sense of community in the classroom, versus asking students that are digital natives and natural born learners to turn off in school.

Online or virtual learning through the use of mobile devices, such as smartphones, is one of the most promising alternative tools for successfully teaching Black males (Laing, 2010). McCoy (2012) suggests that e-learning has the potential to reduce segregation in the classroom based on income and race, increase the possibility that African American male students may choose careers in technical fields, and provide opportunities for African American males to succeed in otherwise hostile environments. It may be that online learning gives Black males a reprieve from socially constructed visual presentations of masculine identity in favor of more intellectual identities to both fellow students and teachers. Freire (1970) acknowledges that teachers are artists who make it possible for students to discover who they are, not who the teachers want them to be.

Online Culture Connects with the Hip-Hop Culture

The website RapGenius.com intersects literature, poetry, and hip-hop lyrics in a collaborative online environment that promotes critical literacy. Connections to hip-hop as a tool for education do not end there. Dr. Christopher Emdin promotes using hip-hop to increase interest in STEM, with the end result of reducing school absences through the use of science-based rap lyrics. Hip-hop, a subculture that has a significant connection to Black male and academic identity, has many icons that break stereotypes that technology is just for geeks. Dr. Dre, T-Pain, Nas, will.i.am, Snoop Dogg, Jay Z, and 50 Cent have all partnered with tech companies and/or started their own tech companies, proving that science not only is cool, but can be profitable. Online learning has the benefit of anonymous communication so that it potentially eliminates stigmas based on race, gender, and sexual orientation.

Using Technology to Raise Expectations of At-Risk Students

Technology can enhance student engagement and productivity. It also increases the complexity of the tasks that students can perform successfully and raises student motivation (Baker, Gearhart, & Herman, 1994; Dwyer, Ringstaff, & Sandholtz, 1990; Means & Olson, 1995). Technology can also help students develop positive cooperative learning relationships, enabling them to work and learn together as they research topics and create presentations. Moreover, students with special needs may require more coaching in computer-based activities, but they will benefit from the experience of learning with other students. Technologies can be used to learn basic skills, but most digital tools have real-world applications that can also help all—including at-risk students—engage in research, design, analysis, composition, and dynamic classroom communication.

One of the leading innovators in classroom technology applications, Dr. Elliot Soloway, has explored how technology will change our expectations of at-risk students' learning capacities. Dr. Soloway is one of the founders of the Center for Highly Interactive Computing in Education and principal investigator of the Center for Learning Technologies in Urban Schools at the University of Michigan. The excerpt below is from a videotaped interview for the video series *Learning With Technology*, program #2, "Tools for Thinking."

> If we follow the naturally mandated guidelines for what classrooms need to look like, we're going to be asking kids to do different kinds of activities than we're asking them to do now. For example, as opposed to reading materials in a book and answering questions at the end of the chapter, what we're going to be asking kids to do is go . . . collect data. We're also going to be asking them to build models of the data that they collect and visualize the data. The only way to do those new sets of activities is to employ technology. Scientists use technology to do those kinds of activities, build models, visualize the data, report on their data, and report on their theories. (North Central Regional Educational Laboratory, 1996)

Five Ways to Use Technology in the Classroom

In a Brookings report (West & Bleiberg, 2013) titled "Five Ways Teachers Can Use Technology to Help Students," coauthors Darrell West and Joshua Bleiberg contend that the American education system has a remarkable resistance to innovation. Although advances in IT have revolutionized how people communicate and learn, schools have not effectively adopted digital tools, they say. To take advantage of new technology, teachers must be shown how these tools can empower them and help their students learn. Below are excerpts from their list of five strategies for successful teacher adoption of education technology:

1. Schools must use technology that empowers teachers. Teachers rightly reject education technologies that divert their attention from instruction. The best

education technologies enable teachers to do more with fewer resources. Communication platforms like Twitter, Facebook, or Tumblr enable dynamic communication with students. Teacher-empowering technologies include mobile apps that grade written student work and provide lesson plan databases. School systems need to aggressively track what works for their teachers and put all other unworkable technologies aside.

2. Teachers should treat the adoption of technology as part of lesson planning. One of the major drivers of bad policy is policy churn. New district leaders want to make their mark adopting new policies and jettisoning the old. This constant changing of priorities makes beneficial reforms difficult to implement. Teachers can incorporate technology directly into their practice and insulate their students from the deleterious effects of policy churn. For example, teachers can use Khan Academy or other online resources to improve remediation. Systematic adoption of technology at the classroom level limits the damage of shifting policy-maker priorities.

3. Teachers should not fear open-source technologies. Many people mistakenly believe that education technologies are expensive and complicated to use. Open-source technologies (denoting software for which the original source code is made freely available and may be redistributed and modified) are stable, secure, and compatible with other platforms. Organizations both small and large use open-source devices every day. Many businesses use open-source servers for their efficiency and cost savings. They often have large communities that provide high-quality customer support. Best of all, open-source technologies often cost less than proprietary products.

4. Use online education portfolios to evaluate students. Educators have known about the benefits of paper-based portfolios for generations. Portfolios allow students to express creativity for difficult-to-assess subjects. Teachers can choose from a variety of online portfolio providers tailored to the needs of their classroom. They also serve as a platform for students to demonstrate growth. Online portfolios have many advantages over paper-based options because they cost less and allow for more robust outreach. Online portfolios are also amenable to a wider variety of formats including video, music, or other interactive features.

5. Teachers should embrace the Common Core State Standards. Common standards make teaching simpler. Teachers have to write lessons that comply with district, state, and national standards. Having a single set of

standards eliminates redundancy and conflicting guidelines. Furthermore, universal adoption of common standards will support future technological innovations that aid teachers. From a technical perspective, standards facilitate the development of new technologies. Innovators can focus on developing tools that better serve students rather than solving technical challenges of interoperability created by multiple sets of standards.

The authors conclude that a lack of school financing limits educators' ability to adopt new education technology in many districts. However, they say that teachers in all school districts can help reform and improve education by adopting technologies that are inexpensive and easy to use.

Advanced Placement and National Writing Project Teachers Document the Digital Divide in the Twenty-First Century

Digital technology, such as greater home broadband adoption and mobile platform ownership, is expanding our capacity to teach and learn anywhere and anytime. Increasingly, school districts are expected to take advantage of this technology to enhance instruction for a generation of students that is already tech oriented. Teachers in higher income communities—with this technology in hand—are empowered and able to raise their standards and expectations accordingly. Educators in low-income communities often cannot set the same standards because they lack comparable technology to leverage the learning environment.

A 2013 Pew survey of AP and NWP teachers documents this digital divide (Purcell, Heaps, Buchanan, & Friedrich, 2013). The following are among the findings:

- 70 percent of teachers working in the highest-income areas say their school does a "good job" providing resources for teachers and they favor incorporating digital tools in the classroom, compared with 50 percent of teachers working in the lowest-income areas.
- 73 percent of teachers of high-income students receive formal training in this area, compared with 60 percent of teachers of low-income students.
- 56 percent of teachers of students from higher-income households say they or their students use tablet computers in the learning process, compared with 37 percent of teachers of the lowest-income students.

- 52 percent of teachers of upper- and upper-middle-income students say their students use smartphones to look up information in class, compared with 35 percent of teachers of the lowest-income students.
- 39 percent of AP and NWP teachers of low-income students say their school is "behind the curve" when it comes to effectively using digital tools in the learning process; just 15 percent of teachers of higher-income students rate their schools poorly in this area.
- 56 percent of teachers of the lowest-income students say that a lack of resources among students to access digital technologies is a "major challenge" to incorporating more digital tools into their teaching; 21 percent of teachers of the highest-income students report that problem.
- 33 percent of teachers of lower-income students say their school's rules about classroom cell phone use by students have a major impact on their teaching, compared with 15 percent of those who teach students from the highest-income households.

Smartphones: An Emerging Learning Platform

A smartphone is a cellular telephone that provides Internet access, digital voice, text messaging, e-mail, still and video cameras, web download capacity for recorded programs, video viewing, and even video chat. Smartphones today are essentially mobile computers. Smartphones also can run downloadable software applications. The cell phone market today is dominated by smartphones. Thus, the rise in the use of smartphones can enable school districts and teachers to provide supplemental education on mobile platforms for students in low-income communities. Ironically, studies have shown that the use mobile phones and computers for education is miniscule compared to their use for entertainment. This *time-wasting gap* is particularly prevalent in poor communities where youth heavily use mobile for Internet access and often have parents who are digitally savvy. Considering the situation, there is an opportunity for teachers in low-income neighborhoods to encourage students to use educational cell phone applications to spend more time on learning activities and less time on social networks and entertainment platforms. Edutopia (Edutopia, 2012), a foundation that tracks trends in educational innovation, is a good resource for both parents and teachers who are looking for information about mobile learning.

Smartphones are Bridging the Digital Divide by Race and Income

According to the Pew Research Center (Smith, 2014), increased Internet adoption and the rise of mobile connectivity has reduced the digital divide for some groups but not all. African Americans in comparison to Whites are less likely to use the Internet and to have high-speed broadband access in the home. Today, seven percentage points separate Black/White Internet usage (87 percent of Whites and 80 percent of Blacks are internet users), and twelve percentage points separate home broadband use (74 percent of Whites and 62 percent of Blacks have broadband connection in the home). However, the rise in mobile device usage is bridging the digital divide, particularly on mobile device platforms (i.e., cell phones and tablets). In contrast to Internet use and broadband adoption, Blacks and Whites are equally likely to own a cell phone of some kind, and they have similar smartphone ownership percentages and similar social networking site usage (i.e., Facebook, LinkedIn or Google Plus), but African Americans have higher levels of Twitter usage than Whites (22 percent of online Blacks are Twitter users, compared with 16 percent of online Whites). Lastly, Whites as compared to Blacks are more likely to own a tablet (34 percent vs. 29 percent) or an e-reader (26 percent vs. 21 percent). All of these "Black/White" technology usage and ownership comparisons are summarized in table 8.

African Americans adults are slightly ahead in smartphone ownership as well as slightly ahead in social media use. Young African Americans are also more likely to use social media (Marketing Charts, 2014). However, these trends of African American digital media and social interaction preferences do not translate into higher levels of classroom achievement.

Teen Mobile Phone Ownership and Social Media

Another Pew Internet research report (Smith, 2013) states that 78 percent or approximately four out of five teenagers (ages twelve to seventeen) own a mobile phone, and more than one out of three teenagers owns a smartphone (37 percent of all teenagers). In contrast to teen ownership of computer desktops, laptops, and tablets, it is important to note that *only* mobile phone technology is bridging the digital divide, since there are only small differences in ownership of smartphones by race, ethnicity, or income. In fact, Black teens and students from poor families

TABLE 8. White vs. Black Digital Technology Usage

ADULT TECHNOLOGY USAGE	WHITE	BLACK
Internet Usage (i.e., accessing the Internet using any device and any location)	87%	80%
Broadband in the Home	74%	62%
Cell phone ownership	90%	92%
Smartphone Ownership	53%	56%
Tablet Computer Ownership	34%	29%
E-Reader Ownership	26%	21%
Social Networking Site Use (e.g., Facebook, LinkedIn, Google Plus)	72%	73%
Twitter Use	16%	22%

TABLE 9. White, Black, Hispanic, Low-income Teen Technology Usage

TEEN TECHNOLOGY USAGE	WHITE	BLACK	HISPANIC	LOW-INCOME
Internet Usage (i.e., accessing the Internet using any device and any location)	98%	92%	88%	89%
Broadband in the Home	74%	64%	53%	54%
Cell phone ownership	81%	72%	64%	69%
Smartphone Ownership	35%	40%	43%	39%
Tablet Computer Ownership	25%	19%	21%	15%
Desktop/Laptop Computer Ownership	81%	64%	79%	73%
Mobile Access to Internet (phone, tablet, etc.)	77%	74%	63%	66%
Access Internet Mostly on their Cell Phone	24%	33%	21%	30%
Social Networking Site Use (e.g., Facebook)	81%	88%	77%	N/A
Twitter Use	23%	39%	19%	N/A

eligible for Title I federal education funding assistance are more likely to mostly access the Internet on their cell phone versus White teens. Furthermore, Black teens are more likely to use Facebook and Twitter than Hispanic and White teens. All of these statistics are summarized in table 9.

How Mobile Technology Can Enhance Reading: A Case Study

The report "Pockets of Potential: Using Mobile Technologies to Promote Children's Learning" (Shuler, 2009), conducted by the Joan Ganz Cooney Center at Sesame Workshop, draws on interviews with a cross-section of research, policy, and industry experts to illustrate how mobile technologies such as cell phones, iPod devices, and portable gaming platforms might be more widely used for learning. Two excerpts from the report explain how some educators have adopted mobile technology to improve reading.

EXCERPT 1: ESCONDIDO UNION SCHOOL DISTRICT'S PROJECT iREAD

A group of pilot teachers in Escondido Union School District are exploring the use of iPod devices, GarageBand, and iTunes to improve student reading. Using the iPod's voice memo and a Belkin recorder, students can record and then hear themselves reading, which improves motivation and helps them work on fluency and comprehension. Teachers can also import student recordings into their iTunes library and create time-stamped digital portfolios (via playlists) that they can use to track progress over time. Data collected from a small group of fourth-graders has found that using iPod devices to practice fluency resulted in more rapid improvement rates compared with a control classroom.

EXCERPT 2: JUMP INTO READING FOR MEANING

JUMP focuses on the development, delivery, and evaluation of a supplemental vocabulary instructional game for the Nintendo DS Lite. The curriculum targets low-performing fourth-grade students enrolled in supplemental educational services programs. The JUMP game is a hybrid vocabulary instructional program and role-playing adventure game designed to teach and assess word-learning strategies and to increase the student's vocabulary through an innovative mix of teaching methods, storytelling, and game play. The game involves exploring 10 diverse environments, overcoming robot challenges, completing engaging quests, and solving thought-provoking puzzles.

The Future of Learning

The impact of mobile devices as a teaching tool that aids teachers in being extra effective in providing online tutorial support and as a learning tool for students in supporting them in the educational achievement goals is tremendous. In this twenty-first century, mobile learning is where teachers and students can now connect using their mobile or wireless device (e.g., laptop, smartphone, and tablet) to teach/learn anytime and anywhere. Mobile learning is the natural evolution of distance learning (i.e., teaching at a distance), and the historical beginning of distance learning dates back to the Industrial Revolution and coincides with the early forms of correspondence schools (Keegan 2005). Desmond Keegan writes that early forms of distance learning were typically individual based and separated the learner from both the teacher and the learning group, and technology was used as a substitute for the teacher. The rise of the Internet in the twentieth century and the digital (electronic) computer ushered in the next evolution of distance learning, which was e-learning (i.e., electronic learning).

Communication and assignment submission by letter correspondence was replaced by the use of the telephone and such digital technologies as the fax machine and e-mail. Thus, e-learning resulted in teacher/student interaction becoming less impersonal and less asynchronous. And in the twenty-first century, with the sales of mobile devices (e.g., smartphones and tablets) far outpacing the sales of desktop and laptop computers, e-learning evolved into mobile learning or m-learning. Now, more than ever, teacher/student interaction could be more personal, information and educational resources more readily accessible, and student learning more self-directed, thus allowing for the possibility of greater academic achievement.

Dr. Sugata Mitra's Hole in the Wall Experiment

Dr. Sugata Mitra, professor of educational technology at Newcastle University, champions a new method of teaching. Mitra has designed an alternative to the traditional methods of public education that have been around since the Industrial Revolution. Calling it a system of self-organized learning environments (SOLE),

EDUCATORS IN THE FIELD

Sugata Mitra, Professor, Educational technology at Newcastle University

Education is a self-organizing system, where learning is an emergent phenomenon

Educational researcher Dr. Sugata Mitra's "Hole in the Wall" experiments have shown that, in the absence of supervision or formal teaching, children can teach themselves and each other, if they're motivated by curiosity and peer interest. In 1999, Mitra and his colleagues dug a hole in a wall bordering an urban slum in New Delhi, installed an Internet-connected PC, and left it there (with a hidden camera filming the area). What they saw was kids from the slum playing around with the computer and in the process learning how to use it and how to go online, and then teaching each other.

The "Hole in the Wall" project demonstrates that, even in the absence of any direct input from a teacher, an environment that stimulates curiosity can cause learning through self-instruction and peer-shared knowledge. Mitra, who's now a professor of educational technology at Newcastle University (UK), calls it "minimally invasive education." In the June 13, 2013 UK publication "The Observer," Dr. Mitra stated the following:

> One of the teachers who works with me said to her class of nine-year-olds: "There is something called electromagnetic radiation that we can't see, can you figure out what it is?" The children huddle around a few computers, talking, running around and looking for clues. In about 40 minutes, they figure out the basics of electromagnetism and start relating it to mobile signals. This is called a self-organized learning environment, a Sole. In a Sole, children work in self-organized groups of four or five clustered around an internet connected computer. They can talk, change group, move around, and look at other groups' work and so on.

At TED2013, Sugata Mitra made a bold TED Prize wish: Help me build a place where children can explore and learn on their own—and teach one another—using resources from the worldwide cloud (Mitra 2013).

Mitra focuses on the use of technology to empower students to maximize both their social and academic capital by giving them the total freedom to pose and answer their own questions. Thus, SOLE creates an academic environment that harnesses the power of cool pose to foster greater academic achievement. Furthermore, Dr. Mitra won the $1 million TED Prize in February 2013 to experiment further with his work and has expanded his methods to schools in India, Cambodia, the UK, and Africa. Education-as-usual assumes that kids are empty vessels who need to be sat down in a room and filled with curricular content. Dr. Mitra's experiments prove that wrong.

The Culmination of Twenty-First-Century Learning

Neuroscience research reveals that student-led learning and collaboration is more aligned with a child's natural way of learning. Recently, *Wired* published the article "How a Radical New Teaching Method Could Unleash a Generation of Geniuses," which detailed a story about a poor rural Mexican school that resides next to the city dump, where on most days a rotten smell drifts through the cement-walled classrooms. The teacher, Sergio Juárez Correa, was used to teaching the typical traditional style of lectures, memorization, and busy work. So after five years, he decided to experiment with a new style of teaching a curriculum by providing "prompts, not answers." This innovative pedagogy involves teachers providing prompts only and not the answer. In this learning environment, teachers are the "guide on the side" and not the "sage on the stage," so that students are able to lead the discussions, and teach and learn from one another. This novel teaching method is creating ways for children to discover their passion—and uncovering a generation of geniuses in the process. Students in class struggled at first, but then they began to learn and teach each other. This method of teaching also taps into new strains of research being conducted by evolutionary psychologists. They suggest that "if you're not the one controlling your learning, you're not going to learn as well." With this philosophy, a small Mexican public school went from being one of the lowest scoring schools in the nation to the highest in only a year. Sergio happened to discover a video describing the work of Sugata Mitra, a professor of educational technology at Newcastle University in the UK. In the late 1990s and throughout the 2000s, Mitra conducted experiments in which he gave children in India access to computers. Without any instruction, they were able to teach themselves a surprising variety of things, from DNA replication to English.

Evolutionary psychologists have also begun exploring this way of thinking. Peter Gray, a research professor at Boston College who studies children's natural ways of learning, argues that human cognitive machinery is fundamentally incompatible with conventional schooling. Paulo Freire also says that modern schooling needs to be more liberating for the learner and less oppressive to students (Freire, 1970). Gray points out that young children are natural learners and motivated by curiosity and playfulness to teach themselves a tremendous amount about the world. And yet when they reach school age, we supplant that innate drive to learn with an imposed curriculum.

> We're teaching the child that his questions don't matter, that what matters are the questions of the curriculum. That's just not the way natural selection designed us to learn. It designed us to solve problems and figure things out that are part of our real lives. (Davis, 2013)

Conclusion

This chapter adds to the emerging research on the use of smartphones to help close achievement gaps of African American males. Helping the educational attainments of Black males is cool in itself. However, using technology for learning can connect with African American males in many different ways, such as using hip-hop to stimulate interest in learning, such as STEM topics in science.

Mobile device technology, particularly smartphones, if used correctly have the potential to help African American males increase their cool factor, that is, assist Black males in balancing their academic identity with their social identity (Ransaw, 2013). However, we do not advocate that Black males should get rid of their masks completely, but to change their masks depending on the circumstance. Sometimes you need a mask to survive on the streets. However, that same mask of self-confidence and bravado may also serve you well on Wall Street, but you need a different type of mask when you are a salesman trying to sell yourself or a prospective employee that is trying to get a job at a marketing firm. Lil Wayne wears a gold chain and gold teeth when he is in a video. But sometimes Lil Wayne takes off his gold chain and gold teeth when he is in a business meeting. Yes, hip-hop is a business, but Jay Z, 50 Cent, Kanye, and Puffy code switch (exchange one mask for another) when they are performing on stage and when they are in the boardroom.

In other words, digital learning environments like smartphones can be looked at as a way to help educators help Black males to remain who they are while still maintaining their masculine and cultural values.

This chapter focused on smartphones to close achievement gaps for African American males. School districts are expected to take advantage of this technology to enhance instruction for a generation of digital natives, and teachers in higher-income communities—with this technology in hand—are empowered and able to raise their standards and expectations. Still, educators in low-income communities often cannot set the same standards because they lack the necessary digital technology tools.

Also, the chapter discussed the shift of the traditional distance-learning paradigm (leveraging desktops) where the learning mantra was "I can learn anytime and any pace" to the twenty-first-century mobile-learning paradigm (leveraging mobile devices) where the learning mantra is "I can learn anytime, any pace, and anywhere." This is because the Internet has created new paradigms of social interaction, and mobile devices provide greater learning, equity, and access to online educational services for students than ever before. Additionally, the latest in neuroscience research on how students learn best reports that student-led learning and collaboration is more aligned with a child's natural way of learning. Finally, the rise in student smartphone ownership is enabling students to take more command of their learning needs. Finally, teachers having high expectations for all of their students will enable educators to provide supplemental, online education to close the achievement gap for all students, particularly African American males.

NOTE

1. The GRPS is currently engaged in resolving a proactive compliance review with the U.S. Department of Education's Office of Civil Rights (OCR) on issues relating to the underrepresentation of African American students in CCP courses, programs, and schools within the district.

REFERENCES

Baker, E. L., Gearhart, M., & Herman, J. L. (1994). Evaluating the Apple Classrooms of Tomorrow(SM). In E. L. Baker & H. F. O'Neil, Jr. (Eds.), *Technology Assessment in Education and Training* (pp. 173-198). Hillsdale, NJ: Erlbaum.

Boykin, A. W. (1983). The academic task performance and Afro-American children. In J. T. Spence (Ed.), *Achievement and achievement motives: Psychological and sociological approaches* (pp. 324–371). San Francisco: W. H. Freeman.

Brown, N., & Fox, M. (2013). *Digital differences: The "haves" and the "have-nots."* Afternoon breakout session, Coaching 101. Dearborn, MI.

Corey, D. L., & Bower, B. L. (2005). The experience of an African American male learning mathematics in the traditional and online classroom—A case study. *Journal of Negro Education 74,* 321–331.

Davis, J. (2013). *How a radical new teaching method could unleash a generation of geniuses.* Retrieved from http://www.wired.com/business/2013/10/free-thinkers/all/.

Dwyer, D., Ringstaff, C., & Sandholtz, J. H. (1990). The evolution of teachers' instructional beliefs and practices in high-access-to-technology classrooms (Paper presented at the annual meeting of the American Educational Research Association, Boston, 1990).

Edutopia. (2012). *How Successful Careers Begin in School.* Retrieved from http://www.edutopia. org/.

Freire, P. (1970). *Pedagogy of the oppressed.* New York: Continuum.

Green, K. (2009). Best practices on how teachers can instill confidences and competence in math students. In R. L. Green (Ed.), *Expectations in education: Readings on high expectations, effective teaching, and student achievement* (pp. 179–202). Columbus, OH: SRA/McGraw-Hill.

Green, R. L. (2009). *Expectations: How teacher expectations can increase student achievement and assist in closing the achievement gap.* Columbus, OH: McGraw Hill.

———. (2014). *Expect the most—provide the best: How high expectations, outstanding instruction, & curricular innovations help all students succeed.* New York: Scholastic.

Green, R. L., White, G., & Green, K. K. (2012). The expectations factor in Black male achievement: Creating a foundation for educational equity. In S. Lewis, M. Casserly, C. Simon, R. Uzzell, & M. Palacios (Eds.), *A call for change: Providing solutions for Black male achievement* (pp. 21–45). Boston: Houghton Mifflin Harcourt.

Judge, S. (2005). The impact of computer technology on academic achievement of young African American children. *Journal of Research in Childhood Education 20,* 91–101.

Keegan, D. (2005). *Mobile learning: The next generation of learning.* Dublin: Distance Education International.

Kukulska-Hulme, A. (2009). Will mobile learning change language learning? *ReCALL 21,* 157–165.

Kyeong-Ju Seo, K. (2013). *Using social media effectively in the classroom: Blogs, wikis, Twitter, and more.* New York: Routledge.

Laing, T. (2010). Virtual learning: A solution to the all-Black male school debate and the challenge of Black male K–12 outcomes. *Journal of African American Males in Education 1*(3), 1–19.

Lee, C. D. (2000). Signifying in the zone of proximal development. In C. D. Lee & P. Smagorinsky (Eds.), *Vygotskian perspectives on literacy research: Constructing meaning through collaborative inquiry* (pp. 191–225). New York: Cambridge University Press.

Mancilla, R. L. (2014). *BYOD: Re-examining the issue of digital equity.* Teachers College Record. Retrieved from http://www.tcrecord.org/Content.asp?ContentID=17639.

Marketing Charts. (2014). 40% of young online African-Americans use Twitter. Retrieved from http://www.marketingcharts.com/online/40-of-young-online-african-americans-use-twitter-39034.

McCoy, K. L. (2012). *A study of African American males and their response to online learning* (Unpublished doctoral dissertation). Capella University.

Means, B., & Olson, K. (1995). *Technology's role in education reform: Findings from a national study of innovating schools.* Washington, DC: U.S. Department of Education, Office of Educational Research and Improvement.

Mitra, S. (2013). Build a school in the cloud. *Ted Talks.* Retrieved from https://www.ted.com/talks/sugata_mitra_build_a_school_in_the_cloud.

Miyake, A., Kost-Smith, L. E., Finkelstein, N. D., Pollock, S. J., Cohen, G. L., & Ito, T. A. (2010). Reducing the gender achievement gap in college science: A classroom study of values affirmation. *Science, 330*(6008), 1234–1237.

NAEP (National Assessmefnt o Educational Progress). (2014). *Results for 2013 NAEP mathematics and reading assessments are in.* Retrieved from http://www.nationsreportcard.gov/reading_math_2013/#/executive-summary.

North Central Regional Educational Laboratory (1996). Captured wisdom: Integrating technology into adult literacy instruction [CD ROM Transcripts]. Oak Brook, IL: North Central Regional Education Lab.

Oakes, J., Joseph, R., & Muir, K. (2004). Access and achievement in mathematics and science: Inequalities that endure and change. In J. A. Banks & C. A. McGee-Banks (Eds.), *Handbook of research on multicultural education (2nd ed.) (pp. 69–90).* San Francisco: Jossey-Bass.

Oakes, J., Rogers, J., Donough, P., Solorazano, D., Mehan, H., & Noguera, P. (2000). *Remedying unequal opportunities for successful participation in advanced placement courses in California high schools.* Unpublished report of the ACLU of Southern California.

Pew Research Center. (2010). Teens and mobile phones. Retrieved from http://www.pewinternet.org/2010/04/20/teens-and-mobile-phones-3/.

Purcell, K., Heaps, A., Buchanan, J., & Friedrich, L. (2013). *How teachers are using technology at home and in their classrooms*. Pew Research Center. Retrieved from http://www. pewinternet.org/2013/02/28/how-teachers-are-using-technology-at-home-and-in-their-classrooms/.

QEM (Quality Education for Minorities). (2010). *Minority males in STEM workshop series report: Executive summary.* Washington, DC: Quality Education for Minorities Network.

Ransaw, T. S. (2013). *The art of being cool: The pursuit of Black masculinity.* Chicago: African American Images.

Root-Bernstein, R., & Root-Bernstein, M. (2011). *Turning STEM into STREAM: Writing as an essential component of science education.* National Writing Project. Retrieved from http://www.nwp.org/cs/public/print/resource/3522.

Shuler, C. (2009). *Pockets of potential: Using mobile technologies to promote children's learning.* New York: Joan Ganz Cooney Center at Sesame Workshop.

Slavin, R. E. (1977). *Student team learning techniques: Narrowing the achievement gap between the races.* Baltimore, MD: John Hopkins University Press.

Slavin, R. E., & Oickle, E. (1981). Effects of cooperative learning teams on student achievement and race relations: Treatment by race interactions. *Sociology of Education 54*, 174–180.

Smith, A. (2014). *African Americans and technology use: A demographic portrait.* Pew Research Center. Retrieved from http://www.pewinternet.org/2014/01/06/african-americans-and-technology-use/.

U.S. Census (2012a). Table 230. Educational attainment by race, Hispanic origin, and sex: 1970 to 2010. Retrieved from http://www.census.gov/compendia/statab/2012/tables/12s0230.pdf.

U.S. Census (2012b). Table 232. Mean earnings by highest degree earned: 2009. Retrieved from http://www.census.gov/compendia/statab/2012/tables/12s0232.pdf.

Vincent, J. (2006). Emotional attachment and mobile phones. *Knowledge, Technology & Policy 19*(1), 39–44.

West, D., & Bleiberg, J. (2013). *Five Ways Teachers Can Use Technology to Help Students.* Pew Research Center. Retrieved from http://www.brookings.edu/research/opinions/2013/05/07-teachers-technology-students-education-west-bleiberg.

Wilkins, A. C. (2008). *Wannabes, goths, and Christians: The boundaries of sex, style, and status.* Chicago: University of Chicago Press.

Woodford, P. F. (1967). Sounder thanking through clearer writing. *Science 156*(3776), 743–745.

Zickuhr, K., & Smith, A. (2013). *Home Broadband 2013.* Pew Research Center. Retrieved from http://www.pewinternet.org/2013/08/26/home-broadband-2013/.

Using Response to Intervention Effectively with African American Males

Sean Williams

The so-called modern education, with all its defects, however, does others so much more good than it does the Negro, because it has been worked out in conformity to the needs of those who have enslaved and oppressed weaker peoples.

—Carter G. Woodson

The reauthorization of the Individuals with Disabilities Education Act (IDEA) of 2004 spurred sweeping changes in how special education students are identified in the United States. IDEA encourages instructional models that are research-based and emphasize the analysis of student progress data prior to special education identification. Response to intervention (RTI) is at the forefront of these models, and it is currently being implemented across the nation. RTI has shown promise not only to support special education students, but also as a benefit to all students. This study will examine how RTI is also a promising program to help close the achievement gap between African American males and White males.

Literature Review

To fully appreciate the implementation of RTI, two understandings are particularly helpful. First, it should be understood that RTI is a policy that is intended to improve the way students are taught basic reading and math skills (Kozleski & Huber, 2010). Through the use of progress-monitoring techniques, students are continually exposed to targeted instructional interventions aimed at closing skill deficits among all students (Batsche et al., 2006). Second, to implement RTI effectively, school leaders must be willing to reevaluate current curricular offerings (Hall, 2007). Implementing RTI programs requires a different approach to how students are instructed, scheduled into courses, and tested throughout the school year (Hall, 2007). Investigating the choices that school leaders made in implementing RTI may help enlighten further issues of overidentification and achievement gaps in future RTI policy designs.

RTI Background

RTI was developed over the past two decades by special education researchers and others to assist with reading and mathematics instruction, although reading is commonly its primary focus. RTI is a systematic method of instruction that requires the use of research-based strategies and frequent progress monitoring of student performance data in order to assist students with specific skill improvements (Shapiro et al., 2011).

Although RTI contains very few new teaching techniques, it does emphasize comprehensive data-collection methods and student progress monitoring to inform ability grouping of students. With an emphasis on remediation of skills, RTI requires teachers to adopt new instructional practices that are more child-specific, as well as to receive targeted training specific to skill remediation (Batsche et al., 2006). These new instructional practices are often perceived by teachers to be at odds with the core curriculum that they are required to teach (King, Lemons, & Hill, 2012; O'Brien & Stewart, 1990, Ratekin et al., 1985). When subject area teachers are asked to teach outside of their areas of expertise, such as teaching basic skills like reading, they tend to resist (Bintz, 1997). This resistance is often attributed to a lack of confidence in teaching outside of their subject area, or to a belief that teaching reading is not their responsibility (Ratekin et al., 1985; O'Brien & Stewart, 1990). The combination of teachers feeling that they have limited time to teach their core content and in some cases resistance to teaching remedial skills such as reading further complicates the implementation of RTI interventions.

Some of the resistance to teaching these much-needed remedial skills may, in fact, be related to the perception of RTI as a special education program. RTI has roots in the 2004 reauthorization of IDEA, which was aimed at reducing the number of special education students (U.S. Department of Education, 2006). Essentially, special education was established in 1975 with the passage of the Education for All Handicapped Children Act (U.S. Congress, 1986). Since then, special education participation has tripled, from 2 percent to 6 percent nationally (Fuchs & Fuchs, 2006).

RTI and General Education Students

RTI is essentially an early-detection model for identifying students who are lagging in skill development in comparison to expected development benchmarks (Brown, 2008; Gersten & Dimino, 2006). Emphasis thus far has been on literacy interventions; however, mathematics is slowly becoming the focus of RTI programming as well. To identify deficiencies, schools categorize student achievement data into three levels using a series of tests (known as *universal screeners*) that evaluate basic skills such as fluency and comprehension. Using this data, students are then divided into three groups based on ability levels. This process of testing and grouping students requires a huge amount of cooperation among school personnel such as administrators, specialists, and teachers. Because many of these tests are given in a one-on-one method, volunteers are usually trained to assist with the testing, and students have to be slotted in for testing appointments. This process requires much planning and staff development. Schools typically devote professional development time to developing an RTI process within the organization.

Tier I

The first level of RTI's tiered intervention is identified as tier I. In tier I, students need some or no academic interventions to maintain grade-level work. This work is often done in core classrooms, and it requires teachers to deliver core curriculum with specific research-based strategies. In many cases, teachers are not asked to teach more content; instead, they are asked to teach their standard content with targeted instructional strategies or methods of delivery.

Tier II

Tier II identifies students who need more specific and intense instruction. This instruction is often delivered to students in small groups, in addition to the instruction they receive in general core classes. Tier II students are sorted through testing data, such as fluency and universal comprehension screeners (tests).

Tier III

Tier III, the final level, consists of students who need the most support. These students typically have a learning disability and require small group or one-on-one instruction, and they receive support using a research-based program designed for their specific deficiencies. For students to move down from one tier to another tier, they must demonstrate proficiency on a variety of targeted assessments (Fuchs & Fuchs, 2006). Student achievement is also continually monitored throughout the year to assure the intervention strategies are appropriate and effective by frequently monitoring the progress of each individual student. By using RTI instructional strategies, classroom teachers become more accustomed to viewing instruction as an individualistic process rather than as a group process. Teachers are more aware of students' academic deficiencies and can adjust their lesson planning throughout the year to help improve academic achievement.

RTI and Supportive Research

Mark Shinn at National Louis University of Chicago is one of the leading researchers studying the impact of RTI. Shinn found that prescribed interventions modified reading instruction, based upon diagnostic testing of student skills, and subsequently diminished the number of students who needed special education services (Shinn, 2007). Shinn found that universal screening is a key practice needed to identify and align individualized interventions for all students. Shinn's examination of κ–5 studies discovered that students make dramatic increases in reading in as little as five weeks with the use of targeted instruction.

Further research involving a meta-analytic study of RTI models illuminated a study by Vellutino, Scanlon, Sipay, Small, Pratt, Chen, and Denckla (1996) that found that first-grade students who participate in RTI not only improve their reading but approach normative levels of reading. This research reinforces the idea that RTI can help to limit the number of students requiring special education services (Burns, Appleton, & Stehouwer, 2005). O'Connor & Freeman (2005) studied approximately eight hundred students who were participating in reading activities provided through tiered interventions and found that students showed improvement in all reading measures. This study also saw a reduction from 15 percent to 8 percent in students being referred to special education for the four years following the study.

Another meta-analysis of RTI found that the earlier student interventions are given, the better students perform on skill assessments. This research was conducted by examining eighteen studies of early reading interventions that took place between 1995 and 2005. Researchers found that these interventions became more effective when they were implemented as early as first grade (Wanzek & Vaughn, 2007). This finding also reinforced evidence that suggests how crucial early interventions can be for children. The younger students are when they receive targeted interventions, the better off they will be as they progress through their education (U.S. Department of Education, 2011).

A study of RTI implementation in six elementary schools found that students who were included in reading activities, such as word identification, word attack, and passage comprehension activities, outperformed on pre- and posttests students who only had traditional classroom instruction (Wanzek & Vaughn, 2007). Looking at literacy specifically, a national study following the progress of 13,609 kindergarten students found that integrating phonics instruction and language arts instruction led to larger gains than those resulting from any one instructional strategy (Xue & Meisels, 2004). Both of these studies demonstrate that early, focused instruction is not only effective but also essential in building strong basic skills that may lead to increased confidence for future learning. This emphasis on early interventions is a key support for RTI. The success of these studies strongly supports the need for interventions for students as early in life as possible.

A Gap in Research

Special education programming is intended for students with disabilities; however, the increased inclusion of minority and low-income students in this programming is a disservice to all students. Minority students may feel inferior when improper placements are made, leading to a more negative attitude toward school. Ladson-Billings (1995) also believes that instruction tends to ignore cultural assets that minority students possess in the absence of culturally relevant curriculum. This absence of cultural relevance to students can attribute to perceptions of education deficits among these students. Additionally, special education services have become diluted for the students they are actually intended for, and minority and low-income students receive services that are not designed for their particular deficiencies (Patton, 1998). In essence, special education services are designed for students who have difficulty learning, not necessarily for students who can learn but have skill deficits influenced by socioeconomic factors.

When students are placed in special education, they can become reliant on the additional help. Teachers also often assume that these students will always need additional help. The assumption of a student's inability to do work creates an atmosphere of inhibited academic success that surrounds the students (Patton, 1998). Delpit (1988) suggests that teachers can interpret a student's lack of success as an issue of the student instead of an issue of the teacher's instructional practices. RTI and early interventions could prevent a student from being placed in special education altogether.

RTI policy is a federal regulation aimed at promoting change in practice at the school level for how students are identified for special education. In IDEA of 2004, federal legislators specified language that expressly permits, but does not require, RTI for identified students with disabilities (IDEA, 2004). This legislation changed the status of the discrepancy model from required to optional, which was the existing process of identifying students who demonstrated a gap between their IQ and academic performance, as measured by testing and academic achievement. The extremely high cost of special education across the nation spurred efforts to find alternative ways to assist students and perhaps prevent them from requiring special education services (Batsche et al., 2006). With this thinking in mind, RTI programming is currently being used as a tool to help reduce the number of special education students across the United States. Under this new legislation, the states can decide if they want to use or prohibit the discrepancy model and use RTI instead (Zirkel, 2009).

It is important to note that while adopting RTI is voluntary, as of 2011, forty-three states allow RTI or other methods of determining special education eligibility, and seven states require RTI (NCRI, 2012). With support from three major education associations, Spectrum K–12 School Solutions conducted a national survey of 1,306 district administrators with the intent to assess the implementation of RTI throughout the United States. The survey found that 94 percent of district administrators indicated that their schools were at some stage of implementation of RTI. Of these district administrators, 24 percent say they have reached full implementation. This report demonstrates that RTI implementation is underway nationally and that implementation is uneven, but it does not necessarily illuminate why these RTI programs have not reached full implementation in each school (Spectrum, 2011).

In IDEA 2006, in addition to the clarification of rules, new flexibility for schools to use special education funds to support general education students within a comprehensive RTI program was made allowable. Broadening the scope of special education intensifies the need to ensure that policy designs are providing the desired outcomes.

Contemporary Application and Viable Focus for Research

Michigan is pushing schools to use RTI through a new accountability program founded on a waiver granted by the federal government, which allows some modifications to No Child Left Behind requirements (MI Dept. of Education Waiver, 2012). The waiver includes a state top-to-bottom ranking of schools, based on achievement, improvement, and achievement gaps. Priority Schools are defined as schools that find themselves in the bottom 5 percent of the top-to-bottom ranking. Priority Schools are required to implement a reform plan that includes targeted research-based interventions for students. These interventions must be correlated to performance data, and the planned teacher professional development must be aligned to support the prescribed interventions.

Additionally, schools identified as Focus Schools must also use similar strategies to narrow the achievement gaps found in their schools. Focus Schools are the 10 percent of Michigan schools that have the most significant achievement gap between the average of the top 30 percent and bottom 30 percent of their students' performances on statewide standardized tests (Michigan Department of Education Focus, 2012). Like Priority Schools, these schools must use research-based interventions. Thus, although RTI is not specifically required to fulfill several state requirements and guidelines, schools must have some RTI or RTI-related programming within their building. With the understanding that schools have limited time and resources, it is highly likely that schools would adopt a uniform system like RTI or multi-tiered system of supports (MTSS) to meet the requirements of these multiple accountability programs.

As schools implement RTI, there is a danger that African American males are overidentified into RTI programs at an excessive rate to their White counterparts. Due to this potential imbalance and the important tool that RTI represents, the relationship between RTI programs in schools and African American males should be studied.

Methodology

To develop a better understanding of the impact of RTI on African American males, new studies should focus on the gaps in student achievement between African American males and White students, as well as the percentage of identification among these subgroups. To collect data for analysis, the focus at the school-level RTI implementation gathered from school administrators most likely will benefit from using a mixed-method design. Additionally, results from future studies using data from school administrators to discern the achievement levels of student subgroups after the implementation of RTI and the administrator's attitudes toward RTI have the potential to close the achievement gap. Closing achievement gaps requires not only the support of parents, teachers, and principals, but the backing of policy makers as well.

Cohen and Hill (2001) found that a key to successful instructional policy implementation at the school level is "substantial professional learning . . . a 'necessary' condition for any improvements in practice" (p. 185). Professional training programs based on these suggestions have the potential to influence the implementation of future RTI programs.

The study as described will take approximately two years to conduct and will require substantial funding. The potential barriers to this study include access and participation to the various stakeholders and the time to process the qualitative and quantitative data collected. However, with the cost in mind, the federal government spent $11.5 billion on special education in the United States in 2007 and $11.9 billion in 2013 (US Department of Education, 2014). Given increasing special education expenditures, a comprehensive RTI policy analysis is justifiable and warranted.

Researchers involved in this proposed study should have extensive experience with RTI as a program, in addition to experience conducting school-level implementation research. We have provided RTI handouts at the end of this book to help increase RTI school-level capacity for both teachers and administrators. RTI expertise benefits the researcher's ability to prioritize focus on high-value elements of the study (Stake, 1970).

By focusing on implementation at the school level, any future study about African American males and achievement gap reductions will have heuristic value if it attempts to identify how RTI affects the achievement gap and the rate of African American male participation. By better understanding the trends in identification and the perceptions of school administrators toward RTI and African American males, this new knowledge may help inform future RTI policy.

REFERENCES

Batsche, G., Elliott, J., Graden, J. L., Grimes, J., Kovaleski, J. F., Prasse, D., Schrag, J., & Tilly, W. D. (2006). Response to intervention: Policy considerations and implementation. Alexandria, VA: National Association of State Directors of Special Education.

Baum, H. S. (2003). *Community action for school reform*. Albany: State University of New York Press.

Bintz, W. P. (1997). Exploring reading nightmares of middle and secondary school teachers. *Journal of Adolescent & Adult Literacy 41*, 12–24.

Brown, J. E., Dolittle, J. (2008). A cultural, linguistic, and ecological framework for Response to Intervention with English language learners. Teaching Exceptional Children *40*(5), 66–72.

Burns, M. K., Appleton, J. J., & Stehouwer, J. D. (2005). Meta-analytic review of responsiveness-to-intervention research: Examining field-based and research-implemented models. *Journal of Psychoeducational Assessment 23*, 381–394.

Charmaz, K. (2006). *Constructing grounded theory: A practical guide through qualitative analysis.* Thousand Oaks, CA: Sage Publications.

Coburn, C. E. (2001). Collective sensemaking about reading: How teachers mediate reading policy in their professional communities. *Educational Evaluation and Policy Analysis 23,* 145–170.

———. (2006). Framing the problem of reading instruction: Using frame analysis to uncover the microprocesses of policy implementation. *American Educational Research Journal 43,* 343–379.

Coburn, C. E., & Talbert, J. E. (2006). Conceptions of evidence use in school districts: Mapping the terrain. *American Journal of Education 112,* 469–495.

Cohen, D. K., & Hill, H. C. (2001). *Learning policy: When state education reform works.* New Haven: Yale University Press.

Cohen, J., Cohen, P., West, S. G., & Aiken, L. S. (2013). *Applied multiple regression/correlation analysis for the behavioral sciences* (3rd ed.). Hoboken: Taylor & Francis.

Creswell, J. W. (2005). *Educational research: Planning, conducting, and evaluating quantitative and qualitative research* (2nd ed.). Upper Saddle River, NJ: Pearson, Merrill, Prentice Hall.

Delpit, L. D. (1988). The silence dialogue: Power and pedagogy in educating other people's children. *Harvard Educational Review 58,* 280–299.

Elmore, R. F. (1979). Backward mapping: Implementation research and policy decisions. *Political Science Quarterly 994,* 601–616.

Fuchs, D., & Fuchs, L. S. (2006). Introduction to response to intervention: What, why, and how valid is it? *Reading Research Quarterly 41,* 93–99.

Gersten, R., & Dimino, J. A. (2006). RTI (response to intervention): Rethinking special education for students with reading difficulties (yet again). *Reading Research Quarterly 41,* 99–108.

Hall, S. L. (2007). *Implementing response to intervention: A principal's guide.* Thousand Oaks, CA: Corwin Press.

IDEA (Individuals with Disabilities Education Improvement Act). (2004). 20 U.S.C. § 1400.

Kansas Department of Education (2009). *Kansas multi-tiered system of supports.* Retrieved from http://www.kansasmtss.org.

King, S. A., Lemons, C. J., & Hill, D. R. (2012). Response to intervention in secondary schools: Considerations for administrators. *NASSP Bulletin 96,* 5–22.

Kozleski, E. B., & Huber, J. J. (2010). Systemic change for RTI: Key shifts for practice. *Theory into Practice 49,* 258–264.

Ladson-Billings, G. (1995). Toward a theory of culturally relevant pedagogy. *American Educational Research Journal 32,* 465–491.

Lipsky, M. (1980). *Street-level bureaucracy: Dilemmas of the individual in public services.* New

York: Russell Sage Foundation.

Michigan. Department of Education. (2011). Response to Intervention: A multi-tiered system of support. Lansing: State Board of Education. Retrieved from http://www.michigan.gov/documents/mde/Response_to_Intervention_362712_7.pdf.

———. (2012). ESEA flexibility waivers summary. Retrieved from http://www.michigan.gov/documents/mde/ESEA_Flex_Waivers_Summary_372801_7.pdf.

———. (2012). Focus schools: Facts and figures. Retrieved from https://www.michigan.gov/documents/mde/Focus_Schools_Facts_and_Figures_394124_7.pdf.

National Center on Response to Intervention (NCRI), (2012). RTI State Data Base.

O'Brien, D. G., & Stewart, R. A. (1990). Preservice teachers' perspectives on why every teacher is not a teacher of reading: A qualitative analysis. *Journal of Literacy Research 22*(2), 101–129.

O'Connor, E. P., & Freeman, E. W. (2005). District-level considerations in supporting and sustaining RtI implementation. *Psychology in the Schools* 49(3), 297–310.

Patton, J. (1998). The disproportionate representation of African Americans in special education. *The Journal of Special Education* 32(1), 25–31.

Ratekin, N., Simpson, M. L., Alvermann, D. E., & Dishner, E. K. (1985). Why teachers resist content reading instruction. *Journal of Reading* 28, 432–437.

Shapiro, E. S., Zigmond, N., Wallace, T., & Marston, D. (2011). *Models for implementing response to intervention: Tools, outcomes, and implications.* New York: Guilford Publications.

Shinn, M. R. (2007). Identifying students at risk, monitoring performance and determining eligibility within response to intervention: Research on educational need and benefit from academic intervention. *School Psychology Review 36*, 601–617.

Spectrum K12 School Solutions. (2011). Response to intervention (RTI) adoption survey 2011. *Global Scholar.* Retrieved from http://www.prnewswire.com/news-releases/2011-response-to-intervention-report-by-globalscholar-nasdse-case-and-aasa-uncovers-latest-trends-in-rti-adoption-among-us-school-districts-128001008.html.

Stake, R. E. (1970). Objectives, priorities, and other judgment data. Review of Educational Research *40*, 181–212.

U.S. Congress. (1986). Handicapped Children's Protection Act of 1986: conference report (to accompany S. 415). Washington, DC: U.S. GPO.

U.S. Department of Education. (2006). Assistance to States for the Education of Children With Disabilities and Preschool Grants for Children With Disabilities; Final Rule. Federal Register, Part II: Department of Education, 34 CRF Parts 300 and 301.

———. (2011). *Nation's report card.* U.S. Department of Education, Institute of Education Sciences, National Center for Education Statistics. Retrieved from http://nces.ed.gov/nationsreportcard/naepdata/.

Vellutino, F. R., Scanlon, D. M., Sipay, E. R., Small, S. G., Pratt, A., Chen, R., & Denckla, M. B. (1996). Cognitive profiles of difficult-to-remediate and readily remediated poor readers: Early intervention as a vehicle for distinguishing between cognitive and experiential deficits as basic causes of specific reading disability. *Journal of Educational Psychology 88*, 601–638.

Wanzek, J., & Vaughn, S. (2007). Research-based implications from extensive early reading interventions. *School Psychology Review* 36, 541–561.

Williams, S. M. (2014). *The principal's role in the implementation of response to intervention* (Unpublished doctoral dissertation). Michigan State University, East Lansing.

Xue, Y., & Meisels, S. J. (2004). Early literacy instruction and learning in kindergarten: Evidence from the early childhood longitudinal study—kindergarten class of 1998–1999. *American Educational Research Journal 41*(1), 191–229.

Yin, R. K. (2003). *Case study research: Design and methods* (3rd ed.). Thousand Oaks, CA: Sage Publications.

Zirkel, P. A. (2009). Legal eligibility of students with learning disabilities: Consider not only RTI but also ß 504. *Learning Disability Quarterly* 32(2), 51–53.

College and the African American Male Athlete

Stephen Brown

> I'm not comfortable being preachy, but more people need to start spending as much time in the library as they do on the basketball court.
>
> —Karim Abdul-Jabbar

The plight of the student-athlete is a unique one. Their college matriculation is a constant battle to maintain a balance between academic success and competitive success. A great deal of criticism and discussion exists regarding the low graduation rates of collegiate athletes, particularly African American males competing in the sport of basketball. Colleges/universities across the country are implementing academic and student-service programs to improve the graduation rates of athletes on their campuses. Unfortunately, these programs are often initiated without gaining an understanding of the student population they are designed to serve.

The Issue at Hand

African American male basketball players historically have the lowest graduation rates of all Division I student athletes (NCAA, 2013).This statistic should be a major

TABLE 1. Graduation Rates—NCAA Division I National Statistics

	2003	2013
All Students	60%	61%
All Student-Athletes	63%	77%
All White Males	*60%*	*61%*
White Male Athletes	60%	77%
White Males—Basketball	52%	76%
All African American Males	*38%*	*41%*
African American Male Athletes	48%	55%
African American Males—Basketball	39%	42%

concern for coaches and athletic directors across the country; however, it seems to go relatively unnoticed. Table 1 lists the graduation rates of all student athletes with an emphasis on the African American basketball players.

The data clearly show a deficit in the graduate rate of the African American athletes as a whole, but even more pronounced is the disparity in the graduation rates between the African American male basketball players and their peers.

There have been several studies and documentaries dedicated to the barriers (i.e., discrimination, isolation, failure to integrate themselves into the campus environment) that African American male basketball players face in their efforts to pursue their undergraduate degree, but very little research if any has been dedicated to examining the experiences of the nearly one-third of African American male basketball players who actually persist to degree completion.

The purpose of this chapter is to shed light on the noncognitive variables and experiential factors and people that had a significant influence on African American male basketball players in Division I programs that persisted to baccalaureate degree completion.

Education has clearly taken a back seat to participation in sports. The public learned about professional athletes who could not read or write, despite having completed their eligibility at well-known colleges (Hawes, 1999). Student-athletes are practicing longer hours and competing in longer playing seasons. Little has been done in many places to treat student-athletes as complete individuals, with academic goals and other needs (Hawes, 1999). Student-athletes are often accepted into colleges and universities with little regard for how well they were prepared for college (Hawes, 1999). As a result, many student-athletes fail to graduate. Low graduation rates have brought new federal legislation requiring institutions to compile and release graduation rates. The government's action prompted the NCAA to adopt a similar measure (Hawes, 1999). Individual school graduation rates became public knowledge, and by the end of the 1990s, some coaching contracts even included bonuses for higher graduation rates (Hawes, 1999). In November 2013, NCAA research verified the fears of many people. Simply because student-athletes received scholarships and competed for the institutions they attended did not mean they graduated. Division I male basketball student-athletes graduated at a rate of 42 percent (NCAA, 2013). These rates are compared to an overall Division I student-athlete graduation rate of 58 percent (NCAA, 2013). For African American male basketball players, the problem is even more alarming. Only 34 percent of Black male basketball student-athletes were graduating (NCAA, 2013).

Theories of Persistence

There have been a number of theories that have attempted to explain the principles of behavioral characteristics and how they affect student persistence. Vincent Tinto has been become one of the most prominent theorists in the area of student persistence.

Tinto's Student Integration Model, one of the most studied models of student persistence, hypothesized that persistence is a result of the interaction between the characteristics of the individual student and characteristics of the institutional environment. The relationship between the characteristics of the individual student and the characteristics of the institution determines the level of commitment to remaining in college (Tinto, 1993).

Tinto defines social integration as compatibility with the university. This social integration can be subdivided into peer group relations and faculty relations. Social integration results from successful adjustment behaviors such as socializing, making friends, and engaging in the social environment of the institution. Academic integration is the "degree of congruency between the intellectual development of the individual and the prevailing intellectual climate of the institution" (Tinto, 1993, p. 118). Academic integration results from the successful academic adjustment behaviors, ones that lead to academic competence and confidence. Tinto believes that academic integration is both the individual's satisfaction with his/her current academic performance and the individual's perception of the potential for future integration.

In his model, Tinto (1993) believes that students come to the educational experience with a certain level of preparedness that involves personal determination to motivation. Students who are unsure of majors, are not well supported by family, or lack good academic preadmission chapter skills are at risk for early departure.

Trends have emerged as part of the noncognitive variables and the precollege/college factors that the participants perceived as dominant factors in their degree completion. A further goal of this chapter is to identify noncognitive variables that had a significant impact on African American males. Noncognitive variables are defined as those variables that are not academic—self-concept of ability, self-confidence, self-esteem, and endurance (Monk, 1998).

Significant Variables

The noncognitive variables that appeared to be most common trends with African American males are career maturity, involvement with the campus community, degree commitment, and other variables such as commitment to family. These variables were identified as playing a statistically significant role in their college matriculation.

Career Maturity

Career maturity can be defined as a fully developed, clearly organized path of career choice, or a legitimate plan to bring to maturity. To this end, career maturity was a variable that stood out among these young men that were able to persist to degree completion. These young men were quite candid in their responses to this question and established a pattern that quickly became apparent to the researcher. For example the participants all had clear, definite career paths and were able to articulate them at an early age.

In short, career maturity played an important role in these young men persisting to four-year degree completion as it appeared that these young men began preparing for their future at an early age. Knowing what you want to do in life, or at least beginning the process of actively thinking about it, inherently begins to charter the course of one's destiny. Although these young men may not have ended up in the careers they saw for themselves early in their lives, the process of thinking about it gave these young men an advantage as they grew older. They had been practicing a skill that many others were unfamiliar with until it was time to make that decision about their career path. As with anything else, the more one practices a certain action the better they are likely to become at it. This does appear to be the case in this instance.

Involvement with the Campus Community

Involvement with the campus community is identified as having the ability/opportunity to interact with and be received by the overall college campus community. This has been identified as a key factor, as the ability to assimilate into the college lifestyle and culture gave them access to avenues that are sometimes unavailable to many student-athletes. This denial of access occurred either due to the time constraints placed on student-athletes or simply because they had been viewed by the college community as not being there for an education and only there to play sports / entertain the student body. Taking this into account, the young men interviewed all had positive interactions with the student body and made several friends outside their usual student-athlete circle. I believe that this interaction was a pivotal moment for these young men, as they were able to relate to other populations of the student body that were more focused on educational endeavors and thus helped to create the studious mindset needed to successfully matriculate through college. Student-athletes' abilities to integrate themselves into their collegiate environment was essential to their overall collegiate success.

Degree Commitment

Degree commitment can be viewed as a level to which an individual is willing to go to ensure completion of their of respective degree. This variable is associated with one's personal resolve. There are a variety of different factors that played a role in these young men's degree commitment, from having a desire to create a better life for themselves and their family to the realization that they were able to get a college degree for free. Whatever their reason, once these African American males actually arrived on a college campus they displayed a tenacity that made their degree completion exceptional.

Commitment to Family

The variable of commitment to family was so obvious that it was almost overlooked by the researcher, but after careful analysis it was clear that there was an impact that was undeniable, as there was not one participant that did not underscore the importance of their family in their educational career. There have been countless accounts of athletes that spoke of promises made to their mothers, fathers, or other significant others that culminated in degree completion. This commitment to family has historically been a strong predictor of not only college completion, but even college attendance in the first place. The perceptions of those closest to these student-athletes have proven to play a very strong role in the choices that are made late in life for these men.

This variable proved to be such a powerful factor that I have chosen to elaborate even further about it and assert a new theory that I've termed Family Attribution Theory that is centered on this phenomenon.

Family Attribution Theory

This theory suggests that there is a phenomenon that African American student-athletes can attribute their persistence to degree completion to their respective families, not always in terms of support, but in terms of a promise/commitment to graduate. There have been countless examples of professional athletes who stated that the reason that they returned to school and finished their degrees was because of a promise made to their mothers or some other family member. Vincent Tinto (1993) touched on commitment in terms of degree commitment, athletic commitment, and institutional commitment, but there is really nothing in the literature outside of basic support (financial and emotional) that begins to explore the many roles and facets of the family on student persistence.

To begin, Family Attribution Theory asserts that in order to achieve collegiate persistence that results in degree completion, student-athletes must possess and experience three essential stages. These attributes are (1) degree commitment, (2) athletic commitment and (3) institutional commitment. At the same time, this theory assumes that the commitment attributes and practices are adaptable in that student-athletes can exercise them as needed given the context/proper circumstances. Second, the theory assumes that the commitment context is comprised of many factors including a significant regard for a particular family member(s), the exposure of the student-athlete by either that family member or some significant person in his life to the collegiate lifestyle, mindset, etc., and constant reinforcement that education is primary with athletics being secondary. Third, Family Attribution Theory recognizes that family members can influence their respective student-athletes and student-athletes can conversely influence their respective family members. Family members, by choosing to exercise their authority, can effectively modify the student-athlete's commitment context by virtue of their legacy and accomplishments. Likewise, student-athletes can influence their family members by causing them to adjust their practices or to gain greater knowledge/competency in a particular knowledge area to enhance their overall influence.

Personal Motivation

These young brothers spoke of several sources that contributed to their personal motivation, and provided some great anecdotes about sources of strength that they drew upon to make their dream of a college degree a reality. Participants all seemed to capitalize on their competitive nature as many stated that they pushed on despite the odds because so few people expected them to succeed. In addition, many participants stated that they knew that a college degree was going to be the key to unlocking a more positive future.

Family Support

Family support is an important variable that cannot be understated in any student's matriculation through college, much less the student-athlete's. Being an African American male student-athlete further exacerbates this need. Family support involves having blood relatives or those considered family to call upon when one's experiences reach a critical need. This support can range from monetary to simple advice. Studies have shown that African American males also viewed support as being able to provide a positive mentor who had already been down the road these young men were trying to travel. These mentors would be able to provide sound advice to these young men, and also provide a very credible source, as they would be speaking from experience. Many times, these young men even in this day and time are first-generation college students, as no one in their family had gone to college before them. Thus, young men having family that had successfully navigated their college matriculation are many times the best support system as they can share from whence they've come and impart knowledge and experiences that no one else in the family may be able to provide. This in my opinion is a critical entity, as the isolation one feels being the only one in your immediate circle attempting something can be crippling.

Athletic Counseling Staff

These young men viewed certain counseling staff as instrumental in assisting them during their college tenure. These young men stated that it was important to have someone familiar with the university system as they were in a vulnerable position during this time and realized the need for someone to intercede on their behalf. There were young men who felt that they did not receive a lot of assistance, but the interviewer realized that this response was somewhat subjective as all of the young men interviewed stated that there was an active athletic counseling department at their respective universities. All sports programs had requirements for student-athletes to interact with this department especially during their freshman year. I perceived that these young men did not have a need to interact with athletic counselors once they had a proper understanding of their educational requirements.

Select Coaches

The litmus test about the effectiveness of coaches is skewed at best. There were several young brothers who stated that their coaches were mainly focused on winning, and focused very little on academics other than making sure players were eligible, but there was also a population that stated that their coaches were very influential in their degree completion. These participants were usually associated with larger institutions with more highly publicized coaches.

Discrimination (Low Expectations)

These young men remained consistent in the fact that many of those involved with their daily academic regimen held low expectations for them as students. Many times, immediate assumptions were made about these young men and their intellectual capabilities the minute they were identified as being a part of the men's basketball team. These young men reported that their professors rarely viewed them as serious students and held the belief that they were not there for an education and more concerned with eligibility rather than matriculation. Several of these young men stated that they were routinely subjected to people who were shocked that they were serious about their academic studies and on track to graduate. It was these low expectations coupled with the young men's almost innate competitive nature, that pushed these young men forward in a quiet defiance to prove these individuals wrong. This was indeed their final act of spite for all of those that ever doubted, disregarded or simply dismissed them as serious students without ever truly knowing who they were as people and the innate drive to succeed that was in them all.

Personal Attitude

Personal attitude played an important role in creating an invisible barrier to the participant's collegiate success. Many of these brothers admitted to struggles with academic motivation, especially after dealing with the rigors of their extracurricular activities. These young men stated that they were required to attend all practices and team meetings, as well as strength/conditioning sessions, and this took a toll on their fatigue levels both physically and mentally. Many spoke of trying to study when they were exhausted from practice or mentally fatigued from watching game film, yet still being expected to perform academically. Another common thread among these men was an admission of laziness when it came to their studies.

Indifference of Coaching Staff

Just as some of these men expressed that their coaches were supportive of their academic endeavors, there was another population that felt that their coaches were simply there to win, and academics was simply a necessary evil for athletic eligibility. These young men stated that at times they were even given ultimatums, asking them choose between athletics and academics.

Financial Considerations

In the midst of all of the other pressures that created barriers for these young men, there were also financial woes to further exacerbate their plight. These young men talked about even having to work part-time to earn money to survive on in addition to all of the other time commitments that they were expected to meet. Luckily, these young men did not fall and are now able to provide a lifeline to the young men who will follow in their footsteps.

The Venn diagram in figure 1 highlights the commonalities of the trends found through research observations and interviews with student-athletes around the country. The left and right sides of the diagram are results from interviews and research observations. These overall trends were the variables and factors that were central themes identified by the participants as most dominant in their persistence to degree completion.

The left side of the diagram indicates the noncognitive variables research stated as the most common predictors to college persistence. The middle section provides the common trends found in the interviews and research observations. The right side of the diagram indicates the precollege/college factors that the participants perceived as dominant factors in their degree completion.

Conclusion

Hamilton (2005) postulated that African American males who succeed in college are viewed as an anomaly. African American male basketball players who succeed in college can then be viewed as an extreme.

This chapter presented a summary of important conclusions drawn from the data presented. It provided a discussion of the implications for action and recommendations for further research in regard to reasons why some African American male basketball players persist to degree completion in Division I institutions.

It is my hope that this research is truly made obsolete in the future, but as it stands currently, this area of research is direly needed. The numbers of African American male athletes continue to climb, as they venture into other areas of athletics and not simply basketball, football, and track and field. There are simply too many young men's lives at stake to take such a lax approach to what most consider an epidemic.

Since I am a former student-athlete, this chapter brought me back to a familiar place and familiar feelings. There were many experiences that we all had in common, some good, some bad, but these experiences helped to shape us into the men we have become today. One common thread that had to be acknowledged in all of the participants interviewed was that of inner strength. All of these men possessed an inner strength that is apparent. There was an inner strength needed

FIGURE 1. Venn Diagram Highlighting the Correlational Factors that Existed between the Noncognitive Variables and the Precollege/College Factors that Were Seen in Each of the Study Participants

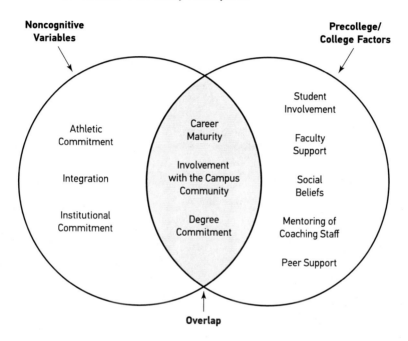

to defy the odds and actually be one of the chosen few to be offered a Division I scholarship, and there was an inner strength in being able to perform at a high level both in the classroom and on the basketball court. This inner strength is the basis of why I felt so compelled to develop this chapter, because all of the young men in question possess this strength.

Whether these men can call upon it when necessary is one different scenario, and whether they are viewing degree completion as something worthy of exerting their strength is yet another. To this end, whose responsibility is it to ensure that these young men seize the golden opportunity that is laid before them in the form of a free education, by most standards the keys to their future and a new life? Is it parental, is it their elementary and secondary educators, is it the coaches that go to the hall of fame and earn merit increases on the shoulders of these young men, or should the responsibility be placed on the university that stands to make millions of dollars in revenue should these men perform the way they are predicted to?

Regardless, there has to be a concerted effort to make sure that these young men are afforded to every opportunity to make the most of their college experience, and this includes leaving it with a college degree. It is up to all of us to ensure that this group of talented, gifted men "Take their best shot!"

REFERENCES

Ashe, A. (1988). *A hard road to glory: A history of the African-American athlete.* New York: Amistad.

Astin, A. W. (1975). *Preventing students from dropping out.* San Francisco: Jossey-Bass.

———. (1982). *Minorities in American higher education.* San Francisco: Jossey-Bass.

———. (1999). Student involvement: A developmental theory for higher education. *Journal of College Student Development 40*(5), 518–529.

Atwell, R. H., Grimes, B., & Lopiano, D. A. (1980). *The money game: Financing college athletics.* Washington, DC: American Council on Education.

AIR (American Institutes for Research). (1989). *Report no. 3: The experiences of Black intercollegiate athletes at NCAA Division I Institutions.* Palo Alto, CA: Center for the Study of Athletics.

Chartrand, J. M., Camp, C., & McFadden, K. (1992). Predicting academic adjustment and career indecision: A comparison of self-efficacy, interest congruence, and commitment. *Journal of College Student Development 33*, 293–300.

Chu, D. (1989). *The character of American higher education and intercollegiate sport.* Albany: State University of New York Press.

Chu, D., Segrave, J., & Becker, B. J. (1985). *Sport and higher education.* Champaign, IL: Human Kinetics Publishers.

Coakley, J. J. (1994). *Sport in society: Issues and controversies* (5th ed.). St. Louis, MO: Mosby.

Delgado, R., & Stefancic, J. (2001). *Critical race theory: An introduction.* New York: New York University Press.

DeFrancesco, C. (1996). Support services for African American student athletes: A case study analysis. *College Student Journal 30*, 2–18.

Eitzen, D. S. (1999). *Fair and foul: Beyond the myths and paradoxes of sport.* Lanham, MD: Rowman & Littlefield.

Erlandson, D. A., Harris, E. L., Skipper, B. L., & Allen, S. D. (1993). *Doing naturalistic inquiry: A guide to methods.* Newbury Park, CA: Sage Publications.

Etzel, E. F., Ferrante, A. P., & Pinkney, J. W. (Eds.). (1991). *Counseling college student-athletes: Issues and interventions.* Morgantown, VA: Fitness Information Technology.

Eulau, H. (1998). *The politics of academic culture: Foibles, fables, and facts.* Chatham, NJ:

Chatham House Publishers.

George, N. (1999). *Elevating the game: Black men and basketball.* Lincoln: University of Nebraska Press.

Hamilton, J. P. (2005). Reasons why African American men persist to degree completion in institutions of higher education. Dissertation Abstracts International, A65 (10), 3717.

Hart-Nibbrig, N. E., & Cottingham, C. (1986). *The political economy of college sports.* Lexington, MA: Lexington Books.

Hawes, K. (1999) *History of the NCAA: The NCAA century series.* The NCAA News.

Haymes, S. N. (1995). *Race, culture, and the city: A pedagogy for Black urban struggle.* Albany: State University of New York Press.

Hoberman, J. M. (1997). *Darwin's athletes: How sport has damaged Black America and preserved the myth of race.* Boston: Houghton Mifflin.

Hopkins, R. (1997). *Educating Black males: Critical lessons in schooling, community, and power.* Albany: State University of New York Press.

Horine, L. (1991). *Administration of physical education and sport programs* (2nd ed.). Dubuque, IA: Wm. C. Brown Publishers.

Hurley, R. B., & Cunningham, R. (1984). Providing academic and psychological services for the college athlete. In A. Shriberg & F. R. Brodzinski (Eds.), *Rethinking services for college athletes* (pp. 51–58). San Francisco: Jossey-Bass.

Knight Foundation. (1993). *Commission on Intercollegiate Athletics* (March 1991–March 1993). Charlotte NC.

Massey, D. S., & Denton, N. A. (1993). *American apartheid: Segregation and the making of the underclass.* Cambridge, MA: Harvard University Press.

Miles, M. B., & Huberman, A. M. (1984). *Qualitative data analysis: A sourcebook of new methods.* Thousand Oaks, CA: Sage Publications.

Monk, T. Y. (1998). *Variables associated with academic achievement of African American males in four-year undergraduate educational institution: A synthesis of studies.* (Doctoral dissertation) Virginia Polytechnic Institute and State University.

Montoye, H. J. (1957). *The longevity and morbidity of college athletes.* Indianapolis, IN: Phi Epsilon Kappa.

Moores, K., & Klas, L. (1989). Comparing personal, social and institutional variables for university dropouts and those who persist. *College Student Journal 23,* 16–22.

NCAA (National Collegiate Athletic Association). (2013). *Official graduation-rates report.* Indianapolis, IN: National Collegiate Athletic Association.

Pascarella, E. T., & Terenzini, P. T. (1991). *How college affects students: Findings and insights from twenty years of research.* San Francisco: Jossey-Bass.

Person, D. R., & LeNoir, K. M. (1997). Retention issues and models for African American male athletes. *New Directions for Student Services*, no. 80, 79–91.

Rossman, G. B., & Rallis, S. F. (1998). *Learning in the field: An introduction to qualitative research.* Thousand Oaks, CA: Sage Publishing.

Sailes, G. A. (1998). *African Americans in sports: Contemporary themes.* New Brunswick, NJ: Transaction.

Seabrooks, J. (2001). *An inquiry of the academic and athletic aspirations of African American student-athletes who participated in Division-I men's basketball* (Unpublished doctoral dissertation). University of Missouri–Kansas City.

Scales, J. (1984). African American student athletes: An example of minority exploitation in college athletics. In A. Shriberg & F. R. Brodzinski (Eds.), *Rethinking services for college athletes* (pp. 71–93). San Francisco: Jossey-Bass.

Sedlacek, W. E. (1987). Black students on white campuses: 20 years of research. *Journal of College Student Personnel,* November, 484–494.

Sedlacek, W. E., & Adams-Gaston, J. (1992). Predicting the academic success of student-athletes using SAT and noncognitive variables. *Journal of Counseling & Development 70*, 724–727.

Sedlacek, W. E., & Webster, D. (1978). Admission and retention of minority students in large universities. *Journal of College Student Personnel,* May, 242–248.

Shriberg, A., & Brodzinski, F. R. (Eds.). (1984). *Rethinking services for college athletes.* San Francisco: Jossey-Bass.

Shujaa, M. J. (1996). *Beyond segregation: The politics of quality in African-American schooling.* Thousand Oaks, CA: Corwin Press.

Smith, R. A. (1988). *Sports and freedom: The rise of big-time college athletics.* New York: Oxford University Press.

Spivey, D. (1983). The Black athlete in big-time intercollegiate sports, 1941–1968. *Phylon 44*, 116–125.

Thelin, J. R. (1994). *Games colleges play: Scandal and reform in intercollegiate athletics.* Baltimore, MD: Johns Hopkins University Press.

Tinto, V. (1993). *Leaving college: Rethinking the causes and cures of student attrition* (2nd ed.). Chicago: University of Chicago Press.

Tracey, T. J., & Sedlacek, W. E. (1987). Prediction of college graduation using noncognitive variables by race. *Measurement and Evaluation in Counseling and Development 19*, 177–184.

Underwood, C. (1984). *The student athlete: Eligibility and academic integrity.* East Lansing: Michigan State University Press.

Yin, R. K. (1994). *Case study research: Design and methods* (2nd ed.). Beverly Hills, CA: Sage Publications.

Using Mentorship to Transition Black Males to Prosperity

Charesha Barrett

I have never had much patience with the multitudes of people who are always ready to explain why one cannot succeed. I have always had high regard for the man who could tell me how to succeed.

—Booker T. Washington

During President Obama's presidency, he developed two initiatives: My Brother's Keeper and the White House Initiative for Educational Excellence for African Americans. These initiatives identified the "opportunity gaps" that are affecting young men of color. History confirms Black males have been facing educational, economic, and political inequities since before the Civil War (Perkins, 2010, p. 2). Even though the Thirteenth Amendment freed Black men from slavery, it did not grant them *true* masculinity. As Black men attempted to build their new identities, they continued to be oppressed—receiving resistance from Whites who were not receptive to the new America. These ongoing struggles not only affected Black men; they impacted Black women. American Black women had to help maintain the economic security for their households because of discriminatory actions against their husbands (Perkins, 2010, p. 3). Black families started investing in Black women's education causing the diminishment in Black men's "patriarchal dominance" (Perkins, 2010, p. 4). These actions over the years have caused Black men to embrace the "negative narrative" that is portrayed in today's society (*My Brother's Keeper*, 2014, p. 4).

In the *My Brother's Keeper Task Force Report*, the committee members list recommendations on how to narrow the "opportunity gaps" for young men of color (*My Brother's Keeper*, 2014). Public, private, and philanthropic organizations along with the National Mentorship Partnership served as advisors on the task force and are working collaboratively to meet the goals of this initiative. The task force concluded that mentorship is the first call to action in ensuring that every young man is maneuvering through the cradle-to-career route.

What is mentoring? This term has evolved over the years, but the National Mentorship Partnership defines it as "a structure and trusting relationship that brings young people together with caring individuals who offer guidance, support and encouragement aimed at developing the competence and character of the mentee" (National Mentorship Partnership, 2005, p. 9). Approximately 17.6 million young Americans are in need of or want mentoring, but only 3 million of them are in quality mentoring programs (Miller, 2014, p. 3). Frederick Douglass once stated that it easier to build strong children than to repair broken men (Tolliver, 2013). Black men are broken. Mentoring has the capacity of making a lasting impact on individuals who do not know their own worth. A study conducted by the Schott Foundation stated, "the social, educational and economic outcomes for black males have been more systematically devastating than the outcomes for any other racial and ethnic group or gender" (Tolliver, 2013, p. 1). Mentorship stresses the vitality of having caring parents and adults in these young men's lives. Stakeholders must collectively work with parents and caregivers to provide them with the necessities to have a seamless transition from childhood to adulthood (*My Brother's Keeper*, 2014). The task force listed five objectives for the mentorship program:

- Entering school ready to learn
- Reading at grade level by third grade
- Graduating high school ready for college and career
- Successfully entering the workforce
- Reducing violence and providing a second chance

Education-Based Mentoring

Education continuously serves as the prevalent barrier that is affecting Black men. During this year's NBA Celebrity All-Star game, Arne Duncan wore the number 80 on his jersey to acknowledge the high school graduation rate reaching 80 percent, the highest in U.S. history. Although this is a major accomplishment for our country and shows improvement, this percentage is disheartening. In 2013, 83 percent of Black students scored below proficient on the National Assessment of Educational Progress (NAEP) in reading, which revealed the urgency of literacy instruction reform. States are currently mandating reading improvement plans to assist struggling readers. These efforts are in place to ensure that all students are proficient in reading by fourth grade. However, the standardized assessments that are associated with these plans contribute to the retention of Black males because of below-level passage rates. Furthermore, there is a correlation between illiteracy and incarceration because 70 percent of the prison population "cannot read above a fourth grade level" (Ellis, 2012). Zero-tolerance policies, expulsions, and suspensions lead to the school-to-prison pipeline.

This "double jeopardy" of being reading deficient and poverty stricken leads to increased dropout rates. Inner-city males are overrepresented in the special education population and experience summer loss due to the lack of home reinforcement. School-based mentoring is essential in breaking the curse because teachers and administrators use mentors as mechanisms to provide support in academic-related activities such as homework assistance, tutoring sessions, and test-taking strategies in reading. In turn, "school-based mentoring is associated with improvements in students' self-esteem, attitude towards school and peer and parental relationships" (Caldarella, Adams, Valentine, & Young, 2009, p. 2). For the older mentees, postsecondary education will become a more realistic option when they receive the support they need to matriculate through school. Four-year degree completion is not an obtainable goal for all mentees; certificate programs and two-year institutions provide other college pathways.

Dr. Shelby Wyatt, a counselor at Kenwood Academy, discussed the importance of the "three E's" in improving the educational outcomes of black males (Wyatt, 2013).

- Evaluation: Assess the students' A-S-K (attitude, skill, and knowledge) deficiencies to determine which barriers (family, school, and community) may prevent them from reaching their lifelong goals.
- Empowerment: Help the students develop their decision-making, communication, and critical-thinking skills.
- Enlightenment: Develop workshops that will help foster their leadership skills (i.e., peer mentoring, conflict resolution).

Career-Based Mentoring

In a country where African Americans only represent a small percentage of the population, the majority of the NBA and NFL players are of this descent. There is something wrong with this picture. Young Black men want to emulate these athletes because of their lavish lifestyles and depictions on television. The reality of these young men attaining this goal is practically impossible. Career-based mentoring can use the mentors' positioning to encourage the mentees to seek alternative career pathways. Middle school is the perfect time to introduce career plans and career assessments. Students need to utilize this time to start planning for their high school and college careers. Big Brothers Big Sisters uses community-based mentoring in its Mentoring Brothers in Action. This initiative includes the Fraternity Brothers, Broadcasting Brothers, and Faith-Based Brothers programs that focus on engaging "African-American men in fraternal, social, faith-based and professional organizations to get involved in one-to-one mentoring to change the odds for African-American boys (BBBS, n.d.). The fraternity collaborative (Alpha Phi Alpha, Kappa Alpha Psi, and Omega Psi Phi) teaches the young men team-building skills, "no is not an option," and the importance of developing postsecondary plans. There are not enough Black males in the teaching field, so they have limited interactions with professional Black men. These mentors can familiarize them with the college and career processes through sharing their own narratives. Since some of these young men have never left the borders of their communities, mentors take them to college tours and career fairs. Mentoring Brothers in Action hosts barbershop recruiting drives and Bowls for Kids' Sake fundraisers to get more African American men to make a long-term commitment to mentoring (National Mentorship Partnership, n.d.).

Anthony Martin, the founder of the Philadelphia-based What It Takes (WIT) program, uses the e-mentoring method to pair at-risk Black male students with successful Black men (Byles, 2012). The online curriculum that is included in this program helps students correspond (asking challenging questions or discussing their thoughts) with their mentors via chat-room-style discussions and e-mail. The mentors respond to the mentees' chat messages by answering questions and providing constructive feedback. This mentoring model affords these professional men opportunities to contribute to their communities without traveling. For the older mentees, it is imperative that mentorship programs establish partnerships with public and private businesses in order to "increase entry-level job, mentorship and apprenticeship options" (*My Brother's Keeper*, 2014, p. 9). These opportunities decrease their likelihood from being permanent students and allow them to gain irreplaceable hands-on experiences. Mentorship does not just apply on the community and school levels; it is essential in providing support for individuals who are transitioning into new positions. Fellowships, internships, and job-shadowing opportunities strengthen their employability skills and promote job stability that results in more earnings (*My Brother's Keeper*, 2014, p. 9).

Health-Based Mentoring

In order to provide for all the needs of the mentees, it is imperative to use a holistic approach. In k–12 schools, guidance counselors are not able to maneuver their students through the college and career processes due to the counselor-to-student ratio and overwhelming schedules. Mentoring programs should collaborate with local counseling, health, and social work agencies to ensure that they address the mentees' physical, emotional, and mental health. Mentors are in compromising situations every day and have to be knowledgeable of crisis procedures. Adolescence is already a turbulent period in a teenager's life; the external pressures may contribute to mental instability. Psychologists and clinical counselors can use their expertise to diagnose and treat psychological problems for the mentees. Peer pressure, gang violence, and self-esteem issues prevent Black males from reaching their full potential. Mentoring programs need to collaborate with dieticians in developing healthy menus and nutrition fairs. HealthCorps, a program created by Dr. Oz, has health coordinators that facilitate mental and physical fitness lessons at schools.

Social workers are important partners because they are able to serve as problem solvers and monitor the young men's living conditions. Obesity is a prevalent problem that is affecting the African American community. Physical health is essential for longevity. The mentors should model "healthy physical habits" through participating in exercise and intramurals.

Mentor/Mentee Pairing

In order to have a successful mentorship program, it is imperative to identify the most appropriate method for pairing of the mentors and mentees. The mismatch between the mentors and mentees is the primary reason that mentorship programs do not succeed (Hilley, 2010). When a person decides to become a mentor, he or she has to be knowledgeable of the time and commitment that is required to make a lasting impact in that mentee's life (National Urban League, 1992). *Child Trends* concluded that mentoring programs "based on a 'developmental' mentoring approach—in which mentors got to know mentees better, were flexible in their expectations of the relationships, and took their cues from mentees about activities—tended to last longer and were more satisfying for both mentor and mentee than programs based on the 'prescriptive' approach, in which mentors viewed their own goals as paramount" (National Mentorship Partnership, 2005, p. 3). Mentors must take into consideration their personal preferences, temperaments, and life experiences and the interests of the mentors and mentees before pairing (National Mentorship Partnership, 2005).

Program Monitoring

The mentor coordinator is essential in ensuring that the program is running smoothly. He/she has the responsibilities of documentation monitoring (i.e., logs) and facilitating bimonthly meetings to provide ongoing support and training for the mentors. In addition, the mentor coordinator, school administrators, and teachers should observe the interactions between the mentors and mentees to determine if they are compatible or not. It is imperative to develop ways to recognize the mentors' and mentees' hard work (i.e., perfect school attendance) (National Mentorship Partnership, 2005, p. 58).

Types of Mentoring

The National Mentorship states the following types of mentorship in its "How to Build a Successful Mentoring Program Using the Elements of Effective Practice" document:

- Traditional Mentoring: one adult to one young person
- Group Mentoring: one adult to up to four young people
- Team Mentoring: several adults working with small groups of young people in which the adult-to-youth ratio is not greater than 1:4
- Peer Mentoring: caring youth mentoring other youth
- E-mentoring: mentoring via e-mail and the Internet (p. 48)

Mentoring Research

- Women typically volunteer to mentor more than men.
- Seniors are more likely to serve as mentors in school-based programs.
- Individuals are hesitant to participate in mentoring programs due to the lack of time and expertise.
- Individuals with higher incomes usually sustain longer in mentoring compared with lower-income individuals.
- College students have trouble committing due to scheduling.
- Married volunteers between the ages of twenty-six and thirty have difficulties in committing to mentoring because of their own family obligations.
- Corporate, municipal, and state employees typically prefer school-based mentoring. These employees probably sustain the program because their employers are committed to the cause.
- Buddy mentoring is an example of a flexible model that allows two mentors to share one mentee. (interpreted from National Mentorship Partnership, 2005, p. 94)

Possible Mentorship Activities

The National Mentorship Partnership suggest the following activities for the mentees (National Mentorship Partnership, 2005, pp. 16–17):

- Field trips
- Menu planning
- Leadership workshops
- Team-Building workshops
- Recreation centers
- Amusement parks
- Concerts
- Picnics
- Parent/family night
- Colleges
- Goal setting
- Museums
- Time management
- Create a resume
- Practice interviewing skills
- Lunch with businesses

Mentorship Program Staff

- Funders
- Advisory committee
- Mentor coordinator
- Caregivers
- Stakeholders

Places to Recruit Mentors

- Local businesses
- Civic organizations

- Churches
- Special interest groups
- Universities and schools
- Fraternities and sororities
- Corporate volunteers (Miller, 2008, B1)

Strategies to Improve Mentor Recruitment

1. Use trained mentees as marketing agents to persuade men to become mentors.
2. Use pictures and stories of single mothers raising boys on brochures and publications. These depictions may "touch the chords of men" and encourage them to serve as positive role models for these young men.
3. Give the mothers of mentored boys and the mothers of male mentors the opportunity to state how this program benefited both parties.
4. Set up a recruitment fair two or three times a year.
5. Use incentives such as free front-row seats to special events or electronic gadgets to encourage male groups to recruit mentors.
6. Use multiple forms of media to recruit mentors on local and state levels.
7. Mentoring should gain support with "clothing stores, car dealerships, athletic clubs, ESPN centers, barber shops" to provide the mentors with discount cards.
8. Encourage the female mentors to recruit the males in their lives to become mentors.
9. Appoint local sports teams to serve as "male recruitment ambassadors."
10. Persuade the male high school and college students to join the program through "community service hours, college course credits and/or stipends for books, gift cards, discounts at eating establishments, clothing stores, sporting events, movies, plays, etc." (Miller, 2008, p. 17).

Recruiting Mentors

Use print media, television, and radio to recruit potential mentors (National Mentorship Partnership, 2005, p. 93).

- Nonprofits
- Local businesses
- Civic organizations
- Churches
- Special interest groups
- Universities and schools
- Fraternities and sororities
- Corporate volunteers

Mentee Recruitment

- Departments of social services or welfare agencies
- Employment and training agencies
- Public and private schools
- After-school programs
- Community centers
- Juvenile detention centers/ex-offender programs
- Drug and alcohol rehabilitation centers

Mentoring Program Training Curriculum

The Mentoring Programs must address the following components in its curriculum (National Mentorship Partnership, 2005, p. 110).

- Program history, mission, and goals
- Program policies and procedures
- Mentor and mentee roles
- Strategies for beginning the match
- Communication skills
- Diversity issues
- Youth development
- How to handle a variety of situations
- Crisis management
- Networks of support

- Child abuse reports
- Community mentoring for adolescent development
- Trainer manual

Mentor Requirements

The National Mentorship Partnership suggests that mentorship should abide to the following requirements when selecting mentors (National Mentorship Partnership, 2005, pp. 107–114):

- Application
- Background check
- References
- Interest questionnaire
- Written response: Personal belief about mentoring
- Written response: What do you anticipate to gain from this experience?
- Meeting with the teacher (if school-based) before mentoring the mentee
- Department of Motor Vehicles check
- Sex Offender Registry check
- Mentor orientation
- Sign the Terms and Conditions of Program Participation

Evaluation Plan

In order to measure the effectiveness of the program, it is imperative to devise an evaluation plan to collect qualitative and quantitative data. In addition, formative (during) and summative (end) assessments should be included to help determine if the program is meeting its targeted goals. The Mentoring Staff should design an evaluation plan that assesses the following areas listed in table.

TABLE 1. Benefits of Formal and Informal Mentoring

	AT-RISK YOUTH AND MENTOR	AT-RISK YOUTH AND NO MENTOR
Planned to Enroll in and Graduate from College	76%	56%
Regularly Participated in Sports Team and Other Extracurricular Activities	67%	37%
Obtained a Leadership Position in a Club, Sports Team, School Council, or Another Group	51%	22%
Regularly Volunteered in the Community	48%	27%

Effects of Mentoring

Mentoring is crucial in ensuring that these young men of color have the fundamental skills to become successful adults. *The Mentoring Effect* report observed the positive outcomes of formal and informal mentoring summarized in table 1 (National Mentorship Partnership, n.d.).

The research on the benefits of mentoring confirms that Black men who receive support from caring adults exhibit prosperity. As we move forward, it is imperative for all stakeholders and public, private, and philanthropic sectors to get involved in ensuring President Obama's mission is fulfilled. Here are some recommendations for broadening the mentorship spectrum (*My Brother's Keeper*, 2014):

- Develop mentorship programs that are addressing the national challenges of men of color.
- Utilize research-based mentoring practices.
- Ensure that all mentorship sessions are purposeful.
- Participate in local, state, and federal policies about mentoring.
- Develop innovative strategies to "close the mentoring gap."
- Recruit more private sectors.

REFERENCES

BBBS (Big Brothers Big Sisters of America). (n.d.). Mentoring Brothers in Action. Retrieved from http://www.mentoringbrothers.org.

Byles, S. (2012). *E-mentoring program aims to reduce dropout rate among Black males.* The Philadelphia Public School Notebook.

Caldarella, P., Adams, M. B., Valentine, S. B., & Young, K. R. (2009). Evaluation of a mentoring program for elementary school students at risk for emotional and behavioral disorders. *New Horizons in Education 57*(1), 1–16.

Ellis, K. (2012). Read or go to jail: Literacy and national reading statistics. Retrieved from http://www.edu-cyberpg.com/Literacy/stats.asp.

Hilley, J. (2010). *The current mentorship model is broken.* Retrieved from http://www. articlesbase.com.

Miller, D. (2008). *Man up: Recruiting & retaining African American male mentors.* Baltimore, MD: Urban Leadership Institute.

My Brother's Keeper Task Force. (2014). *My Brother's Keeper task force report to the president.* Retrieved from http://m.whitehouse.gov/sites/default/files/docs/053014_mbk_report.pdf.

National Mentorship Partnership. (n.d.). *The mentoring effect: Young people's perspectives on the outcomes and availability of mentoring.*

———. (2005). How to build a successful mentoring program using the elements of effective practices. Alexandrria, VA: MENTOR/National Mentoring Partnership.

National Urban League. (1992). *Mentoring young Black males: An overview.* New York: National Urban League Inc. Youth Services.

Nguyen, M., Bibo, E. W., & Engle, J. (2012). Advancing to completion: Increasing degree attainment by improving graduation rates and closing gaps for African-American students. *The Education Trust.* College Results Online.

Perkins, L. M. (2010). The Black gender achievement gap: A historical perspective. *The Claremont Letter 4*, 1–5.

Tolliver, E. (2013). Mentoring—It works for African-American males. *Tri-State Defender*, 21 March.

Wyatt, S. T. (2013). *The brotherhood:Eradicating the prison pipeline through lifelong learning strategies.* National Mentoring Partnership.

Turning Negatives into Positives

Cool Ways to Implement Successful Expectation Violations in Black Male Classrooms

Theodore S. Ransaw, Richard Majors, and Mikel D. C. Moss

I sit in your class, I play by the rules. I'm young, I'm fly, I'm black. So of course I think I'm cool.

— S. G. Flake, *You Don't Even Know Me*, 2010

Due to conflict and cultural miscommunication including nonverbal communication, Black men historically have been misunderstood. Watzlawick's first axiom states that a person, cannot not communicate (Watzlawick, Beavin Bavelas, & Jackson, 1967). In other words, everything we do communicates a message—whether we intend it to or not. Communication occurs even when we are silent. For students, silence can be a form of communicating disengagement from schooling, or it can express embarrassment from not understanding instruction. Both powerful and moving, silence can be just as effective as verbal expressions. Either way, whether verbal or nonverbal, we all communicate. So when a teacher says that a student "just sits there, with no communication whatsoever," the student is in fact communicating. By being aloof, detached, and silent, many Black males are engaging in a *cool pose* as a form of resistance to oppression (Majors & Billson, 1992). This silent stoicism has also been described as the *cool factor*: a behavior that Black males adopt as a way to balance their social capital with their academic capital by not appearing too nerdy or too dumb—just cool (Ransaw, 2013). This cool behavior, which intersects race, class, and gender (Wilkins, 2008) is often adopted as a masculine shield against teachers, the majority of whom—90 percent—are White (Ladson-Billings, 2005). Acting cool is an expressive form of cultural and gendered identity that is typically a nonverbal form of communication and can be misinterpreted as antagonistic.

Taking on a cool pose can sometimes be interpreted as wearing a mask or hiding one's identity, which is perceived by some as negative. This idea that using a mask as a coping strategy is unhealthy could not be further from the truth. Langley & Langley (1983) said "The purpose of masks is always to reveal rather than to conceal" (p. 224). So by these young men showing you their cool pose, they are actually giving you a huge glimpse into who they are, and—more importantly—what they are made of. Warren and Grainger (2000) add even more support to the argument that a cool pose is a way in which Black males shield themselves against oppression with their assertion of the "Mask Principle," which states: "Concealing in order to reveal, the process whereby we strike at the heart of something by deliberately turning our attention elsewhere" (p. 85).

Overview

Many Black males learn to display a cool pose because they feel disconnected in the classroom because teachers do not know how to communicate with them. To provide context regarding this connection, Black students represent close to 18 percent of children in preschool programs, but they comprised 42 percent of preschool students who are suspended more than once (CBS News, 2014). Additionally, most of the suspensions of all Black students between 2009 and 2010 were for minor offenses such as behavioral offenses, wearing unauthorized clothing such as a jacket, or even wearing a hat backwards (Resmovits, 2014; Majors & Billson, 1992). In other words, Black students are more likely to be suspended for nonviolent offenses such as being disruptive or truancy than are White students (Fabelo et al., 2011). Various degrees of punishment and sanctions underpin all teacher/staff interactions with students and immediately erect an insurmountable barrier if the student does not comply in the required way (Majors et al., 2011). Suspension rates of African American males are a reason for concern because school suspensions frequently lead to underachievement, juvenile detentions, future arrests, and limited employment opportunities. This increasing trend of nonviolent offenses that result in school suspensions mirrors the increasing trend of nonviolent offenses that result in incarceration. For example, in 2011, two-thirds of youth in detention are being held for nonviolent charges (Campaign for Youth Justice, 2012). While the overrepresentation of African American males being placed on suspension and in juvenile detention is common knowledge, what is not common knowledge is that suspension disparities start as early as preschool (CBS News, 2014). If behavior, not violence, is the reason that Black students between the grades of 6 and 12 have been suspended at a rate of 43 percent compared to 16 percent of their White peers and expelled at a rate of 13 percent compared to 1 percent of their White peers (Aud & Fox, 2010), misalignment of behavioral expectations are likely to be the cause. While the majority of the offenses that result in suspension are nonviolent, a historical predisposition to fear violence from Black males exists (Bogle, 2000; Hall, 1993). Post–Civil War era history points directly to the reasons behind the relationship between Black men and violence. Alexander states:

> Rumors of a great insurrection terrified whites, and blacks increasingly came to be viewed as menacing and dangerous. In fact the current stereotypes of black men as aggressive, unruly predators can be traced to this period when whites feared that an angry mass of black men might rise up and attack them or rape their women. (2010, p. 28)

These sentiments, while they may have diminished in intensity, have not dissipated completely and have turned into generational learned subconscious behaviors that negatively affect young Black men. While this quote speaks specifically to the lives of Black men in America, evidence of this exists historically and currently in nations that have a long history of colonization in countries where brown-skinned people are in abundance. This generational learned subconscious behavior puts Black and other brown-skinned men at a disadvantage before they even step into the classroom.

Since the majority of the teachers in the United States are White female teachers (Kunjufu, 2002; Ladson-Billings, 2005) and African American males are overrepresented in school suspensions and suspensions for nonviolent offenses, in essence the United States is experiencing expectation violations between White teachers and Black male students at a massive rate. As Brown and Davis (2000) assert, schools are clearly not meeting the social and developmental needs of

African American males. White, middle-class female teachers have a very difficult time understanding and appreciating the cultural norms of other diverse groups. However, is it possible that these behavioral expectations are based on cultural misperceptions and not racism? Bowles and Gintis (1976) assert that schools have a hidden curriculum that creates cultural impasses by promoting White middle-class culture as superior and normal. What *is* normal behavior? Normal behavior is based on what is considered proper (Glasser, 1984), and what is considered proper and normal is based on Eurocentric behaviors and values.

Cool in the Classroom

Communication impasse is a prime factor in determining teacher-student relationships, often to the point of complete breakdown. But teachers are frequently trained to see the problem as lying within the student and readily fall back on punishment and sanctions rather than analyzing and reflecting on their emotions and reactions to a young person's different acts of defiance. Too often, it is the teacher who escalates the tension (e.g., what they say and how they say things), which damages the teacher-student relationship and contributes to emotional and physical stress (Majors et al., 2011). Our young Black men, even with all the emotional baggage and generational trauma they bring to the classroom with them, are still learning and developing the skills and tools needed to navigate this world. One would assume that a teacher, even a young one, would have a firmer grasp on their emotive state and how it translates into the classroom, but we already know that is not true. The fact is little attention has been paid to the emotional literacy of the teachers, teaching assistants, and other school staff who interact with those young people every day. In our view, teachers need to achieve a better balance between "hard" skills such as subject knowledge and cognition or "soft" skills and "relationship based approaches" such as emotionally literacy (Majors et al., 2011).

For example, why it is that Black males are perceived as the hardest to teach instead of White teachers being perceived as the most difficult to learn from? (Pigott & Cowen, 2000). White-based norms of behavior are a salient point to remember especially when we consider that *White* male behavior is hardly considered hostile, angry, and dangerous, but *Black* male behavior almost always is (Delpit, 2006). For this reason, many African American males feel that the school is not a welcoming place and immerse themselves into a state of being that affirms their identity: cool pose (Majors & Billson, 1992). Cool masculine behaviors are comprised of being resilient and acting relaxed, confident, and emotionally detached as a source of strength and power (Hecht, Jackson, & Ribeau, 2003). It is no wonder that males turn to coolness as a strategy to navigate their world and establish their distinct sense of masculinity, as a place to be resilient, and as a source of strength and power (Connor, 1995). This formation of coolness is nurtured in school from a source of ethnic identity that takes place outside of White culture. When people say they do not see color, they may miss the purpose of the cool in regard to both emotional and psychological factors that are necessary to exist in a world based on White norms. Tatum (2005) argues that teacher-training programs do not prepare teachers to navigate the complexities of Black identity and culture.

For this reason, scholars in several disciplines have been advocating the inclusion of culture in regard to positive education outcomes for African American males (Ladson-Billings, 2005, 2009; Delpit, 2006; Kunjufu, 2002; Howard, 2006). Educators have also considered the role of positive expectations in regard to improved student performance (Baksh & Martin, 1984). However, a critical look specifically at the role of cultural expectation violations in regard to improving the educational outcomes of African American males is a new concept as far as we know. We feel that a better understanding of teacher and student interaction through the lens of expectation violations can decrease negative perceptions and suspensions of Black males as well as increase educational outcomes for them.

Expectation Violation Theory

Expectation Violation Theory (EVT), first advanced by Burgoon (1978) and then later revised by Afifi and Metts (1998), asserts that emotional reactions to social situations center around outcomes based more on expectations than on reality. We extend EVT to include misalignments between student and teacher interactions often based on misinterpreted cultural decoding of masculine behavior we call acting cool.

There are two parts to EVT: *predictive* interpreted behavior based on prior experience, and *prescriptive* behavior based on prescribed general social norms. These two actions, predictive and prescriptive, can have both positive and negative expectation violations. An example of a negative student expectation violation is when a teacher corrects a student paper rather harshly because she was unfamiliar with the cultural terms or references of the author. A positive expectation violation is when a teacher gives a high five or a fist bump to a student as a form of reinforcement when he did not expect it. Negative expectation violations can result in many obstacles in the classroom such as a Black male students' reluctance to ask for help for fear of being racially, genderedly, or culturally misunderstood. Positive expectation violations have the potential to increase self-efficacy and motivation for both students and teachers. EVT divides negative and positive expectation violations into two categories, negative valence and positive valence. Negative valences describe expectation violations that are perceived as unfavorable while positive valences are expectation violations that are received positively. Valences, both positive and negative, are evaluations of interactions based on perceptions, and perceptions are influenced by cultural aspects such as race, class, and gender.

Race can be classed, and class can be raced, and race can be gendered like a matrix (Bettie, 2003). We take that to mean that race, class, and gender are not individual lenses that we look at the world through separately. Rather race, class, and gender are interconnected multiple frames of reference similar to a prism that intersects differently resulting in many different perspectives. We assert that the congruence of race, class, and gender in regard to positive expectation violations is the key to success in the classroom for African American students, especially in regard to help-seeking behavior.

Negative Valence and Help-Seeking Behavior

Help-seeking behavior, or "behavior of actively seeking help from other people" (Rickwood et al., 2011, p. 4) can take place differently depending on the culture, especially classroom culture. Classroom norms and expectations are important in regard to recognizing the difference between student frustration levels based on learning styles. While most teachers allow questions at the end of a lesson or allow for questions after new material is presented, help-seeking behavior diminishes when instructional climates view interruptions of the teacher during instruction as unfavorable (Nelson-Le Gall & Jones, 1991). Because of social conditioning, African American students are more likely to seek help from small cooperative groups where they are comfortable challenging explanations, requesting justifications, and being supported with challenging engagement (Nelson-Le Gall & Jones, 1991). Help-seeking behavior that utilizes social supports is a natural part of the process for adolescents who prefer informal rather than formal sources of help (Sheffield, Fiorenza, & Sofronoff, 2004). Additionally, Degruy (2005) asserts that teachers who have the most success working with many students of color emphasize building strong relationships based on mutual trust and respect.

Understanding teacher expectations can reduce student anxiety and behavioral problems, especially when those problems stem from students not understanding instruction and not understanding how to ask for help. Teachers may find success in presenting themselves in a way in which Black male students can ask for help in a way that affirms their masculinity, that is, doesn't make them look weak or foolish. Black male masculinity is especially crucial to remember since there are both racial and gender stigmas to Black males' social status when they ask for help from White female teachers. Additionally, both Black and White teachers utilize more positive nonverbal interactions with White students than with African American students (Pigott & Cowen, 2000). Awareness of this classroom trend among teachers is a crucial step to understanding why Black males may be less inclined to ask for help from authority figures.

> Each actor in the classroom—teacher or student—assigns meanings to the objects, events, and persons at hand, and individual plans of action evolve on the basis of these assigned meanings. An awareness of this processual nature of classroom interaction is a prerequisite for full teacher effectiveness in the classroom setting. (Baksh and Martin, 1984, p. 342)

Help-seeking behavior requires trust and a thorough understanding of relationship/role behavior expectations. Help-seeking behavior works at least two ways. First, teachers are more likely to have higher expectations for students who ask for help. Second, students and teacher have to figure out ways that demonstrate help-seeking behavior in ways that teachers recognize as help-seeking behavior that is not disruptive and uncomfortable.

However, not all students know what appropriate help-seeking behavior looks like to teachers. An assertive style welcomed outside of the classroom may be viewed as threatening or as problem behavior inside of the classroom (Pigott & Cowen, 2000). It is crucial to remember that help-seeking behavior may be displayed differently in different cultures and may even have negative implications depending on its valence. Different perceptions of appropriate help-seeking behavior is especially troubling for African American boys because asking for help from a White female teacher can be read as the epitome of uncool by other boys (Cleveland, 2011). In addition, in key transitional years such as the move from elementary school with one teacher to junior high that has multiple teachers, many students have to learn what expected help-seeking behavior looks like for every different teacher. Around third grade, classrooms switch from being cooperative as well as personalized and become more focused on achievement and competition—the same curriculum period in school where African American achievement levels start to drop (Nelson-Le Gall & Jones, 1991).

Based on unfavorable suspension rates and overrepresentation in special education, it is not illogical to assume that students learn accepted help-seeking behavior based on what is *not* accepted behavior more so than what *is* accepted help-seeking behavior. Research indicates that teachers with low expectations for African American students invest in them less (Pigott & Cowen, 2000).

It is no wonder that many Black male students feel more emotional safety from social networks and lean more toward seeking help from their peers. While expectation violations can be based on race, class, and gender, students also have an additional variable to their education outcomes of just trying to understand what they should be experiencing when they are trying to learn.

It is sometimes difficult for students to recognize they do not understand and need help (Dweck, 2013). For example, a student can read the text out loud flawlessly and not comprehend the meaning of the text. The student may be able to understand the text and not be able to articulate the textual pronunciations when read aloud.

This is not always the case. As students grow older and wiser, it becomes easier to know when they are being misunderstood because of cultural misunderstandings. However, confusion stemming from identifying that you are not being misunderstood because of cultural misunderstanding or because they have missed something else can be troublesome the younger you are. In this regard, culture can be a barrier or bridge in interpersonal interactions. To successfully work with students in a culturally competent way requires teachers to work within the student's cultural context (Campinha-Bacote, 2002). Spitzberg (2000) adds that as communicator motivation, knowledge, and skills increase, communicator competence also increases. The combination of these elements leads individuals to perform confidently in their encounters. Teacher expectations play a large role in how we view ourselves in relationship to how we see our students, and that perspective can change the educational outcomes of our students (Delpit, 2006).

In other words, teachers, like all of us, have blind spots. "The eye only sees what the mind is prepared to see" (Potter, 2007, p. 241). When we focus only on what we expect to see, we fail to see anything else that fits outside of our preconceived notions. Since teachers have the impression that African American students have more deficits than their White counterparts, both African American teachers and White teachers judge African American students to have lower competencies than White children (Pigott & Cowen, 2000). Black male students who continuously adhere to a task without success despite the availability of other strategies such as help-seeking behavior may be hiding failure due to lack of self-confidence and not a deficit in cognitive ability (Nelson-Le Gall & Jones, 1991).

Similarly, a student may be a physical learner who elucidates better when he stands up and walks around when he has an idea. However, when that happens he suddenly becomes a student who lacks discipline. A student who stares off into space because he does not understand the instruction or is a visual learner and is mapping out a process in his head instantly becomes a student who lacks focus. A student who appears to not pay attention because he is constantly turning around to talk to other students becomes identified as a problem child. However, it has been shown that how we process and retain new information is helped by adding movement to the process.

Simple biology supports an obvious link between movement and learning. Oxygen is essential for brain function, and enhanced blood flow increases the amount of oxygen transported to the brain. Physical activity is a reliable way to increase blood flow, and hence oxygen, to the brain (Jensen, 2005). Behavioral problems associated with Black males may be attributed to misaligned cultural norms of kinesthetic learning. In general, teachers indicate African American students are perceived to have more behavioral problems and lower academic performance than White children (Majors, 2001). The reasoning behind this phenomenon is based in part on research that indicates that teachers interpreted child behavior based on social-cultural perspectives and expectations (Pigott & Cowen, 2000; Helms, 2003).

When students feel that they cannot reach their teachers' expectations, help-seeking behavior diminishes and may turn into avoiding help-seeking behavior. Students do not always regard high standards of performance set by their teachers as appropriate or achievable and therefore reject them (Gallahar, 2009). In other words, the necessity of having high academic expectations for student success has been talked about for years (Green, 2009; Lemov, 2010; Ozturk & Debelak, 2005). However, high academic expectations alone are not enough.

Not Just High Expectations Alone

We have assumptions that the more positive teacher expectations are the higher the students' educational outcomes. The truth is that both students with low assessments and top-performing students have concerns about unrealistic teacher expectations. Baksh and Martin (1984) assert that students who are low performing feel unjustifiably pressured by their teachers to do better when they feel they do not have the ability or when they work to the best of their ability and do not achieve desired scores. High-performing students are under lots of pressure and feel that they have to frequently outperform their peers in order to stay ahead (Baksh and Martin, 1984). High-achieving Black male students are likely to not apply to higher level four-year institutions despite having the indicators that they would be successful (Hoxby & Turner, 2013). In fact, many high-achieving African American students tend not to take advanced placement classes and honor classes for fear of more difficult classes affecting their grade point averages. Many high-achieving African American students tend to focus more on grade point average instead of mastery of content (Hoxby & Turner, 2013). African American students who focus on mastery are more likely to ask for detailed answers, seek complex responses to questions, and prefer help that allows them to figure out solutions on their own (Nelson-Le Gall & Jones, 1991).

African American students who have a low intrinsic orientation to mastery show no clear preference for one type of help over the other (Nelson-Le Gall & Jones, 1991). By looking at the classroom as a setting where the perceptions of all of the actors, especially students, are included, teachers can negotiate positive expectation levels with their students (Gallahar, 2009). Recognizing that coolness can be a form of resilience and strength (Connor, 1995), especially for students who do not feel connected to teacher expectations, is the first step in understanding that expectations can have both positive and negative results. The distinction of the term is crucial to this chapter. Educators often recognize cool, but few teacher take the time to analyze the reason behind cool behavior or its socially constructed function, nature, and purpose (Majors & Billson, 1992). This requires a new line of thinking and a paradigm shift. Keeping in mind race, gender, and class while working with students while being cognizant of our own race, class, and gender can be a challenge. However, Ladson-Billings (1995) would call this just good teaching.

So what is good teaching and how does it relate to EVT and Black males? Research indicates that successful Black student and teacher interactions are a result of positive expectation violations. Kunjufu (2002) asserts that the classroom represents the first time many White females have close interactions with Black males. Every conversation is an opportunity to establish a positive relationship with a Black male student. When you are experiencing difficulty with a Black male ask yourself this question: How much do I really know him? If you do not know what his interests, hobbies, or likes and dislikes are, then how can you connect with him?

Increasing Positive Interactions with Black Males

Below are listed some activities designed to help improve relations and foster a deeper sense of understanding between teachers and students.

Relationships

Academia often makes African American males feel unwanted unless they play sports. Because of negative preconceived notions, many African American males lack opportunities to make strong connections with teachers. Consequently, Black male students do not even expect their teachers to care about them at all. One way to counter that is to do what is not expected, in other words exceed expectations by actively seeking and forging relationships with the Black males in your classroom. In studies related specifically to African American college students, Allen (1992) suggests that academic achievement is highest for students who have positive relationships with faculty. This is consistent to Kim's findings (2004) where she asserts that when students participate in research projects with faculty they are more likely to secure a bachelor's degree. We take this to mean that close relationships with educators are key to fostering positive expectation violations and impactful educational outcomes.

Building on Strengths and Interests

African Americans have few opportunities to see role models in science, technology, engineering, and mathematics (STEM), science, technology, engineering, arts, and mathematics (STEAM), and science, computers, robotics, engineering, arts and mathematics (SCREAM) classes. They also very rarely see cultural affirmations in their science textbooks or lessons. Consequently, African American males have little in-school reinforcement in learning the hard sciences and even fewer expectations of educational science spaces as affirming. Dr. Christopher Emdin has created opportunities for positive science-based expectation violations with Science Genius. Science Genius was created to help students who would otherwise not be interested see themselves as scientists. Science Genius started as a way to engage students from ten New York City high schools through hip-hop. Dr. Emdin and a few of his graduate students worked with one class per school, one day per week to teach basic science concepts. The high school students then had a science rap battle that went from best in class to best in school to best in the city. The winner got to call himself a Science Genius for a year. Attendance for the year increased. "Kids relate best when they're standing up," he said (Christopher Emdin, in John Leland, 2014, p. 1). "The teacher can measure engagement by the hand gestures and head bobs. And when the last kid couldn't finish his verse, everybody gave him encouragement. In a traditional school, he'd have failed. We need to expand the notion of what success is" (Christopher Emdin, in John Leland, 2014, p. 1).

Use Enabling Texts

Dr. Alfred Tatum has an answer to the statement "These kids just don't want to read." He asserts that two things combine to describe why Black males are not engaged in classroom texts: lack of interest in the text, and lack of requisite skill and strategies for independent reading of the text (Tatum, 2008). Engaging students with texts that are relevant to their lives and affirm their identity and giving entry into texts before reading is a key way to convey your expectations to Black male readers (Hughes-Hassell & Hitson, 2013).

Gendered and Culturally Relevant Texts

Dr. Thomas Bean and Dr. Theodore Ransaw argue there are at least two contrasting perspectives regarding gender and literacy. One perspective is that schooling is patriarchal, restrictive, and limiting to women and their efforts to function as full participants in a male-dominated working world. The other perspective is that because of the overwhelming amount of White middle-class female teachers in

American schools, education has become feminized for boys (Bean & Ransaw, 2013). Bean and Ransaw advocate for more culturally and gender-enabling texts that appeal to African American males by affirming their identities and interests—in other words culture- and gender-appropriate books are cool.

Some Other Cool Tips That Support Help-Seeking Behavior When Working with Black Males

- Stand in the same place when presenting instruction or new information.
- Avoid distracting background noise when presenting new information, and indicate that you will leave space for questions at the end.
- Use beginning and ending audio clues like a chime when presenting new information.
- Allow students to work in small groups after presenting new material for informal peer questioning (Cleveland, 2011).

This chapter made the case that Black males adopt a cool persona as a form of psychological protection against cultural nihilism, as a way to help balance social and academic capital, and as help-seeking behavior. However, cool is often misinterpreted as defiance, disengagement, and detachment or related behavioral problems. This misalignment between acting cool and help-seeking behavior is largely a result of negative teacher expectation violations. We base this notion on the fact that the majority of teachers in the United States are White middle-class female teachers (Kunjufu, 2002). Our intention was to first identify the reasons for and construction of cool in the classroom, provide an overview of negative and positive expectation violations, and help educators to identity help-seeking behavior. We then provided a few ideas that help mitigate help-seeking behavior in school. Another that may strengthen the relationships between teachers and students is drama therapy.

Drama Therapeutic Activities/Considerations

The North American Drama Therapy Association (NADTA) defines drama therapy as "the intentional use of drama and/or theater processes to achieve therapeutic goals" (NADTA, 2014). Drama therapy is active and experiential. This approach can provide a context for participants to tell their stories, set goals and solve problems, express feelings and emotions, or achieve catharsis. Through drama, the depth and breadth of inner experience can be actively explored and interpersonal relationship skills can be enhanced. Participants can expand their repertoire of dramatic roles to find that their life roles have been strengthened.

Drama therapy lends itself to a variety of different situations, places, and people for the purpose of creatively assisting in and moving through issues that present themselves. Drama therapy is a natural fit for undoing conflict between teachers and Black male students.

Within the drama therapeutic system there exists a growing number of practitioners who are not only utilizing established systems in ways that are beneficial to our young Black men, but are creating new and more culturally relevant and competent models to understand Black males. For example, Smith's (2012) writings on how a drama therapeutic rites-of-passage program can help heal the emotional wounds of Post Traumatic Slave Syndrome can be applied to help Black males solve issues in the classroom. Also, Mikel Moss is establishing a new drama therapeutically based system to address the areas of emotion regulation and emotional literacy in adolescent and young adults dealing with depression, anxiety, post-traumatic anger, stress, etc.

Drama therapy helps to foster the community positive regard that is vital to the success of young Black men in the classroom as we mentioned above. It is vital that the teacher strike a balance between relating to them on a personal level and maintaining a position of authority as well as establishing the role of a sturdy adult in their lives (Smith, 2012). The following activities look specifically at establishing relationships. It is important to note that appropriate disclosure in a teaching environment is vital to relational connections with students of color (Smith 2012). The following activities look specifically at how to establish relationships with youth and Black males. These games allow an opportunity for all participants to open up and share something about themselves as a way of seeing similarities that exist and thus beginning to form bonds that are later on helpful in the classroom and give the teachers vital information they can use in the future to continue to cement the relationships with their student.

An important part of this is buy-in and participation from everyone including the teacher. The teacher serves as a model and sets the tone. Also, drama therapeutically speaking, students are more likely to buy into an activity if the activity leader takes the time to establish a relationship by affirming student identity. Appropriate disclosure is a safeguard not just to allow students and teachers to begin to establish relationships, but also to keep a professional and working distance at the same time. One doesn't have to delve into one's personal history, but facts about hobbies, favorite TV shows, favorite music, etc. can bridge the divide effectively.

Now that we have just discussed and described some of the essential components of drama therapy, we would now like to introduce some activities for working with Black males that have proven to be successful.

Taking on the Roles and Role Training with Black Males

While not something that can be done as an activity for the whole class, role training is something that can be practiced to help a student and a teacher reframe the expectations so that the student and teacher are as successful as possible. The best way to describe role training is to take a role that already exists and optimize it. For instance, instead of saying to a student who is a poor reader that may have behavioral issues as a result, "I think you are going to be the best reader in the class," or "if you just buckle down you can do this." Say to them "I know you can do this, I have faith in you" (and actually mean it!). It's essential that we instill hope and belief in our students whenever possible by role training them to behave better through positive relationship building and regard utilizing the transferential connection that we have begun to establish (Smith, 2012).

Positive Triangulation

In this instance, we will use something that is normally construed as a negative situation and make it a positive situation. Once a week/month take time out to call home and report on something your students did well. All too often the phone call home is a negative thing. How wonderful would it be for the parents to hear something good about their child? Positive phone calls home give an opportunity to solicit more buy-in from the family regarding the education of their son, making yourself available to the parents should they have any questions or concerns about their child or if they need to report anything that would be helpful for their educational process. You are more likely to get some sort of buy-in from a parent if you are calling to report something good than if you are calling to report something bad. Smith (2012) reports that this activity also helps to create a behavior you want to see by enforcing the positive behavior with the parent.

REFERENCES

Afifi, W. A., & Metts, S. (1998). Characteristics and consequences of expectation violations in close relationships. *Journal of Social and Personal Relationships 15*, 365–392.

Alexander, M. (2010). *The new Jim Crow: Mass incarceration in the age of colorblindness*. New York: New Press.

Allen, W. R. (1992). The color of success: African-American college student outcomes at predominantly White and historically Black public colleges and universities. *Harvard Educational Review 62*, 26–45.

Aud, S., & Fox, M. A. (2010). Status and trends in the education of racial and ethnic groups. Washington, DC: National Center for Education Statistics.

Baksh, I. J., & Martin, W. B. (1984). Teacher expectation and the student perspective. *The Clearing House 57*(8), 341–343.

Bean, T. W., & Ransaw, T. (2013). Masculinity and portrayals of African-American boys in young adult literature: A critical deconstruction and reconstruction of this genre. In B. J. Guzzetti and T. W. Bean (Eds.), *Adolescent literacies and the gendered self: (Re)constructing identities through multimodal literacy practices* (pp. 22–30). New York: Routledge.

Bettie, J. (2003). *Women without class: Girls, race, and identity*. Berkeley: University of California Press.

Bogle, D. (2000). *Toms, coons, mulattoes, mammies & bucks: An interpretive history of Blacks in American films* (3rd ed.). New York: Continuum.

Bowles, S. & Gintis, H. (1976). *Schooling in capitalist America*. London: Routledge and Kegan Paul.

Brown, M. C., & Davis, J. E. (Eds.). (2000). Black sons to mothers: Compliments, critiques, and challenges for cultural workers in education. New York: Peter Lang.

Burden, P. R. (1995). *Classroom management and discipline: Methods to facilitate cooperation and instruction*. White Plains, NY: Longman.

Burgoon, J. K. (1978). A communication model of personal space violations: Explication and an initial test. *Human Communication Research 4*, 129–142.

Burgoon, J. K. (1995). Cross-cultural and intercultural applications of expectancy violations theory. *Intercultural Communication Theory 19*, 194–214.

Campaign for Youth Justice. (2012). *Key facts: Youth in the justice system*. Washington, DC: Campaign for Youth Justice.

Campinha-Bacote, J. (2002). The process of cultural competence in the delivery of healthcare services: A model of care. *Journal of Transcultural Nursing 13*, 181–184.

CBS News. (2014). *Black students more likely to be suspended–even in preschool*. Retrieved from http://www.cbsnews.com/news/

education-department-black-preschoolers-more-likely-to-be-suspended/.

Cleveland, K. P. (2011). *Teaching boys who struggle in school: Strategies that turn underachievers into successful learners.* Alexandria, VA: ASCD.

Connor, M. K. (1995). *What is cool? Understanding Black manhood in America.* New York: Crown.

Degruy, J. (2005). *Post traumatic slave syndrome: America's legacy of enduring injury and healing.* Baltimore: Uptone Press.

Delpit, L. (2006). Lessons from teachers. *Journal of Teacher Education 57,* 220–231.

Dweck, C. (2013). *Changing mindsets, motivating students with Carol Dweck.* Webinar Education Week. Retrieved from http://www.edweek.org/media/2012-02-16_changingmindsets.pdf.

Leland, J. (2012). *A hip-hop experiment. The New York Times.* November 16.

Fabelo, T., Thompson, M. D., Plotkin, M., Carmichael, D., Marchbanks, M. P., & Booth, E. A. (2011). *Breaking schools' rules: A statewide study of how school discipline relates to students' success and juvenile justice involvement.* College Station: Public Policy Research Institute, Texas A&M University.

Flake, S. G. (2010). *You don't even know me: Stories and poems about boys.* New York: Hyperion/ Jump at the Sun.

Gallahar, T. M. (2009). *Students' perceptions of teachers' expectations as predictors of academic achievement in mathematics* (Unpublished doctoral dissertation). University of Alabama, Tuscaloosa.

Glasser, W. (1984). *Control Theory—A New Explanation of How We Control Our Lives.* New York: Harper and Row.

Green, R. L. (2009). *Expectations: How teacher expectations can increase student achievement and assist in closing the achievement gap.* Columbus, OH: McGraw Hill.

Hall, R. E. (1993). Clowns, buffoons, and gladiators: Media portrayals of African-American men. *Journal of Men's Studies 1,* 239–251.

Hecht, M. L., Jackson, R. L., & Ribeau, S. A. (2003). *African American communication: Exploring identity and culture* (2nd ed.). Mahwah, NJ: Lawrence Erlbaum Associates.

Helms, J. E., (2003). Racial identity in the social environment. In P. B. Pedersen & J. C. Carey (Eds.), *Multicultural counseling in schools: A practical handbook* (pp. 44–58). Boston: Allyn and Bacon.

Howard, G. R. (2006). *We can't teach what we don't know: White teachers, multiracial schools* (2nd ed.). New York: Teachers College Press.

Hoxby, C., & Turner, S. (2013). *Expanding college opportunities for high-achieving, low income students.* Stanford: Stanford Institute for Policy Research discussion paper 12-014.

Hughes-Hassell, S., & Hitson, A. (2013). *Are you prepared to meet the literacy needs of African American male youth?* Retrieved from *www.learnnc.org/lp/media/uploads/2013/05/ afamlitwebinar.pdf.*

Jensen, E. (2005). *Teaching with the brain in mind.* (Rev. ed.). Alexandria, VA: Association for Supervision and Curriculum Development.

Kim, M. M. (2004). The experience of African-American students in historically Black institutions. *Thought and Action 20*(1), 107–124.

Kunjufu, J. (2002). *Black students, middle class teachers.* Chicago: African American Images.

Ladson-Billings, G. (1995). But that's just good teaching! The case for culturally relevant pedagogy. *Theory into Practice 34*, 159–165.

Ladson-Billings, G. (2005). The evolving role of critical race theory in educational scholarship. *Race Ethnicity and Education, 8*(1), 115–119.

Langley, D. M., & Langley, G. E. (1983). *Dramatherapy and psychiatry.* London: Croom Helm.

Leary, J. D. (2005). *Post traumatic slave syndrome: America's legacy of enduring injury and healing.* Portland, OR: Joy DeGruy Publications.

Lemov, D. (2010). *Teach like a champion: 49 techniques that put students on the path to college.* New York: John Wiley & Sons.

Majors, R. (Ed.). (2001). *Educating our black children: New directions and radical approaches.* New York: Routledge.

Majors, R., & Billson, J. M. (1992). *Cool pose: The dilemmas of Black manhood in America.* New York: Lexington Books.

Majors, R., Cook, S., & Read, D. (2011). *Emotional literacy.* Retrieved from http://www. rightsideofthecurve.com/articles/articles/social-emotional-needs/emotional-literacy.

McCalman, C. L., & Madere, C. M. (2009). Sub-Saharan African students' experiences, perceptions, and expectations with American health services: An intercultural challenge. *Interpersona: An international journal on personal relationships 3*, 156–176.

NADTA (North American Drama Therapy Association). (2014). *What is drama therapy?* Retrieved from http://www.nadta.org/what-is-drama-therapy.html.

Nelson-Le Gall, S., & Jones, E. (1991). Classroom help-seeking behavior of African-American children. *Education and Urban Society 24*, 27–40.

Ozturk, M. A., & Debelak, C. (2005). Setting realistically high academic standards and expectations. *Essays in Education 15*. Retrieved from http://www.usca.edu/essays/ vol152005/ozturkrev.pdf.

PCCY (Public Citizens for Children and Youth). (2000). *Court watch 2011-2012.* Philadelphia: Public Citizens for Children and Youth. Retrieved from http://www.pccy.org/wp-content/

uploads/2014/07/PCCYCourtwatch2012.pdf.

Pigott, R. L., & Cowen, E. L. (2000). Teacher race, child race, racial congruence, and teacher ratings of children's school adjustment. *Journal of School Psychology, 38*(2), 177–196.

Potter, G. (2007). *The white bedouin*. Springville, UT: Council Press.

Ransaw, T. S. (2013). *The art of being cool: The pursuit of Black masculinity*. Chicago: African American Images.

Resmovits, J. (2013). School "discipline gap" explodes as 1 in 4 Black students suspended, report finds. *HuffPost: Blackvoices*. Retrieved from http://www.huffingtonpost.com/2013/04/08/ school-discipline-gap- _n_3040376.html?utm_hp_ref=black-voices&ir=Black%20Voices.

Rickwood, J., Pan Yuen, H., Martin, C., Hughes, A., Baksheev, G. N., Dodd, S., & Yung, A. R. (2011). Does screening high school students for psychological distress, deliberate selfharm, or suicidal ideation cause distress—and is it acceptable? *Crisis: The Journal of Crisis Intervention and Suicide Prevention 32*(5), 254–263.

Sheffield, J. K., Fiorenza, E., & Sofronoff, K. (2004). Adolescents' willingness to seek psychological help: Promoting and preventing factors. *Journal of Youth and Adolescence 33*, 495–507.

Smith, A. (2012). *Stony the road we trod: Implications for drama therapy treatment of post traumatic slave syndrome* (Unpublished master's thesis, Drama Therapy Program). New York University.

Spitzberg, B. H. (2000). A model of intercultural communication competence. In L. A. Samovar & R. E. Porter (Eds.), *Intercultural Communication: A Reader* (9th ed.) (pp. 375–385). Belmont, CA: Wadsworth.

Spitzberg, B. H., & Cupah, W. R. (1989). *Handbook of interpersonal competence research*. New York: Springer.

Tatum, A. W. (2005). *Teaching reading to Black adolescent males: Closing the achievement gap*. Portland, ME: Stenhouse.

Tatum, A. W. (2008). Toward a more anatomically complete model of literacy instruction: A focus on African American male adolescents and texts. *Harvard Educational Review 78*, 155–180.

Wald, J. & Losen, D. (2003). Defining and redirecting a school-to-prison pipeline. In J. Wald & D. J. Losen, (Eds.), *Deconstructing the school-to-prison pipeline*, New directions for youth development 99. San Francisco: Jossey-Bass.

Warren, M., & Grainger, R. (2000). Self-disclosure and disguise: Dramatherapy and masks. In *Practical approaches to dramatherapy: The shield of Perseus*. London: J. Kingsley.

Watzlawick, P., Beavin Bavelas, J., Jackson, D. (1967). Some Tentative Axioms of Communication.

In *Pragmatics of Human Communication: A Study of Interactional Patterns, Pathologies and Paradoxes*. New York: W. W. Norton.

Wilkins, A. C. (2008). *Wannabes, goths, and Christians: The boundaries of sex, style, and status.* Chicago: University of Chicago Press.

Appendix

This section includes handouts intended to help close achievement gaps for African American males. These handouts were created from both research and personal experience. Though most of them correspond to chapters in the book, many can correspond to other chapters, as well. For example, the "RTI Effective Teacher Survey" handout associated with "Using Response to Intervention Effectively with African American Males" may also be of interest to educators with mentorship programs who are looking for support understanding Common Core standards. People who are concerned with peer pressure may find the handout titled "Students of Color Self-Efficacy Handout" useful to their work. It is our hope the handouts in this appendix will help improve your practice and support your goals to foster connection with your students.

REFERENCES

C4EO (2011). *Effective classroom strategies for closing the gap in educational achievement for children and young people living in poverty, including white working-class boys*. London: Centre for Excellence and Outcomes in Children and Young People's Services.

Compton-Lilly, C. (2004). *Confronting racism, poverty, and power: Classroom strategies to change the world*. Portsmouth, NH: Heinemann.

Cooper, E. J. (2005). It begins with belief: Social demography is not destiny. *Voices from the Middle 13*(1), 25–33.

Doll, J. J. (2010). *Teachers' and administrators' perceptions of the antecedents of school dropout among English language learners at selected Texas schools* (Unpublished doctoral dissertation). Texas A&M University.

Dweck, C. S. (2000). *Self-theories: Their role in motivation, personality and development*. Philadelphia: Psychology Press.

Epstein, J. (1995). School/family/community partnerships: Caring for the children we share. *Phi Delta Kappan 76*(9), 701–712.

Gibson, H. V. (2010). *Improving academic achievement for Black male students: Portraits of successful teachers' instructional approach and pedagogy*. Cambridge: Harvard University.

Flaxman, E. (2003). *Closing the achievement gap: Two views from current research*. Eric digest ED482919. Retrieved from http://www.ericdigests.org/2004-3/gap.html.

Green, R. L. (1977). *The urban challenge—poverty and race*. Chicago: Follett.

———. (1987). *Expectations: Research implications on a major dimension of effective schooling*. Cleveland, OH: Cuyahoga Community College.

———. (1998). *Ownership, responsibility and accountability for student achievement*. Dillon, CO: Alpine Guild.

———. (2009). *Expectations: How teacher expectations can increase student achievement and assist in closing the achievement gap*. Columbus, OH: McGraw Hill.

———. (2014). *Expect the most provide the best: How high expectations, outstanding instruction, and curricular innovations help ass students succeed*. New York: Scholastic Books.

Green, R. L., White, G., & Ransaw, T. (2012). *Early warning signs of potential dropouts: What can be done?* Las Vegas: Clark County School District.

Harris, M. D. (1992). Africentrism and curriculum: Concepts, issues, and prospects. *Journal of Negro Education 61*, 301–316.

HB 2722 Advisory Committee. (2008). *A plan to close the achievement gap for African American Students*. Olympia, WA: Office of Superintendent of Public Instruction.

Henderson, A. T., & Mapp, K. L. (2002). *A new wave of evidence: The impact of school, family, and community connections on student achievement: Annual synthesis 2002*. Austin, TX: National Center for Family and Community Connections with Schools.

Hu, H. (2007). To close gaps, schools focus on black boys. *The New York Times*, April 9.

Irvine, J. (1990). *Black students and school failure*. Westport, CT: Greenwood.

Jackson, Y. (2011). *The pedagogy of confidence: Inspiring high intellectual performances in urban schools.* New York: Teachers College Press.

Jackson, Y. & McDermott, V. (2012). *Aim high achieve more: How to transform urban schools through fearless leadership.* Alexandra, VA: ACSD.

Koopelman, K. (2013). *Understanding human differences: Multicultural education for a diverse America,* 4th ed. Boston: Pearson.

Kunjufu, J. (1990). *Countering the conspiracy to destroy Black boys,* vol. 3. Chicago: African American Images.

———. (2009). *How to improve the academic achievement in African American males.* Chicago: African American Images.

Lai, J. & Bishil, D. (2005). *A review of effective district practices used nationwide to close the achievement gap.* Program Evaluation and Research Branch Planning, Assessment, and Research Division Report No. 263. Los Angeles: Los Angeles Unified School District.

Lewis, S., Simon, C., Uzzell, R., Horwtiz, A., & Casserly, M. (2010). *A Call for change: The social and educational factors contributing to the outcomes of Black males in urban schools.* Washington DC: The Council of Great City Schools.

Ransaw, T. S. (2013). *The art of being cool: The pursuit of Black masculinity.* Chicago: African American Images.

Slavin, R. E., & Madden, N. A. (2006). Reducing the gap: Success for all and the achievement of African American students. *The Journal of Negro Education* 75(3), 389–400.

Urban Education Network of Iowa. (2003). *Strategies' for closing the achievement gap.* Des Moines: The Urban Education Network Iowa..

WestEd. (2006). *Charter high schools closing the achievement gap: Innovation in education.* Jessup, MD: U.S. Department of Education.

White, H. E. (2009). "Increasing the achievement of African American males." *Report from the Department of Research, Evaluation, and Assessment 3.* Virginia Beach City Public Schools.

Woolley, M. E. & Grogan-Kaylor, A. (2006). Protective family factors in the context of neighborhood: Promoting positive school outcomes. *Family Relations 55,* 95–106.

Students of Color Self-Efficacy Survey

■ **DESCRIPTION.** Not all students realize that being smart takes hard work and that learning can be accumulated.

■ **OBJECTIVES.** To help teachers pinpoint stumbling blocks their students may not have realized and to open informed discussion for both student improvement and engagement.

■ **OUTCOMES.** A better understanding how your students process their learning ability and what motivates their engagement.

■ **DIRECTIONS.**
1. Have your students fill out the self-survey anonymously.
2. Use the survey trends to inspire adaptations in teaching practices and classroom environment.
3. Re-administer the survey after three months. (*Feel free to make adjustments based on your classroom needs.*)
4. See if improvements correlate to assignments and tests.

1.	I believe that it is cool to be smart.	Y / N
2.	I feel good when I get a good grade.	Y / N
3.	I feel bad when I get a bad grade.	Y / N
4.	I am more interested in learning than getting good grades.	Y / N
5.	Sometimes I hide the fact that I do not understand.	Y / N
6.	I believe smart people do not have to work hard.	Y / N
7.	I think the more time I spend on homework the higher my grades will be.	Y / N
8.	I feel that my teacher(s) cares about me.	Y / N
9.	I feel that my teacher(s) knows when I do not understand.	Y / N
10.	I like to answer questions out loud in class.	Y / N
11.	I like it when the teacher asks me to do math on the board.	Y / N
12.	It is important to me that I look good in front of my friends.	Y / N
13.	I believe that I can ask the teacher(s) questions when I need help.	Y / N
14.	I feel that if I try hard enough I can get it.	Y / N
15.	When I read, it is easy for me to tell when I do not understand.	Y / N
16.	When I answer a math problem, it is easy for me to tell when I do not understand.	Y / N

17. I did well in reading this year.   **Y / N**
18. I did well in math this year.   **Y / N**
19. My teachers give me more good compliments than bad.   **Y / N**
20. My teachers make me feel that I can understand the lesson most of the time.   **Y / N**
21. I understand what it takes to do well in school.   **Y / N**
22. I understand how to use math in everyday life.   **Y / N**
23. I understand the steps it takes to get to college.   **Y / N**

Teachers of Students of Color Self-Efficacy Survey

■ **DESCRIPTION.** Teachers often benefit from self-reflection of their internal beliefs and how they may influence their teaching practices.

■ **OBJECTIVES.** To help teachers pinpoint areas of focus to improve teacher-student relationships.

■ **OUTCOMES.** A better understanding how teacher reflections can inform beliefs and influence student relationships.

■ **DIRECTIONS.**
1. Fill out the survey honestly.
2. Use survey results to inspire adaptations in teaching methods and classroom environment.
3. Re-administer the survey after three months. (*Feel free to make adjustments based on your classroom needs.*)
4. See if adjustments correlate to higher scores on assignments and tests.

1. My students believe that it is cool to be smart.	Y / N
2. It is important for my students to look good in front of their friends.	Y / N
3. My students are more interested in learning than in getting good grades.	Y / N
4. Sometimes my students hide the fact they do not understand.	Y / N
5. My students believe smart people do not have to work hard.	Y / N
6. My students know the more time they spend on homework the higher their grades will be.	Y / N
7. My students feel good when they get good grades.	Y / N
8. My students feel bad when they get bad grades.	Y / N
9. My students know when they do not understand.	Y / N
10. My students are comfortable asking me questions when they need help.	Y / N
11. My students feel that if they try hard enough they can learn.	Y / N
12. When my students read, it is easy for them to realize when they do not understand.	Y / N
13. My students like to answer questions out loud in class.	Y / N
14. My students like to do math on the board.	Y / N
15. My students feel I care about them.	Y / N
16. My students feel that I get them.	Y / N

17. My students feel that I understand their culture.   **Y / N**
18. My students feel that I understand their language.   **Y / N**
19. I make my students feel as if they can understand the lesson most of the time.   **Y / N**
20. I give more good compliments than bad.   **Y / N**
21. My students understand what it takes to do well in school.   **Y / N**
22. My students understand how to use math in everyday life.   **Y / N**
23. My students understand the steps it takes to get to college.   **Y / N**

Best Practices for Closing the Achievement/Relationship Gap of African American Males

■ **DESCRIPTION.** There are many research-based examples of schools and districts that have successfully helped to improve educational outcomes for African American males. Below are a sampling of successful ideas categorized by grade level. This handout is a great discussion starter for professional development sessions.

■ **OBJECTIVES.** To offer educators a quick guide of best practices and research based tips in an easy to read format.

■ **OUTCOMES.** A handy resource to create and evaluates school improvement strategies to close achievement gaps for African American males.

■ **DIRECTIONS.**
1. Look over this best practices guide in and around your classroom. (Grade levels can vary across districts as well as states, and some of these tips can be used for other grades.)
2. Implement the practices that best suit your school, building, or district to close achievement gaps for African American males.

Pre-K/Kindergarten

1. Keep in mind that adopting new curricula does not, in general, produce large improvements in learning outcomes. Changing teaching practices, through extensive continuing professional development, is the most powerful classroom strategy for closing attainment gaps.
2. Use structured phonics instruction, cooperative learning, frequent assessment, and teaching metacognitive skills (e.g., "learning to learn"), which can significantly raise outcomes.
3. Use structured phonics-based approaches, which in general work better than nonphonics approaches.
4. Offer reading circles and encourage working in smaller groups.
5. Provide parental material promoting parent advocacy and student nutrition.
6. Suggest parents ask their child three things they learn each day.
7. Suggest that parents who may be unable to listen to their children read before bedtime record their kids' reading to monitor progress.

8. Share best practices with other teachers in the school.
9. Finance teacher cultural awareness, African drumming, poetry, etc.

Elementary School

1. Provide rigorous curriculum with strong emphasis on STEM areas and language development.
2. Expand Mathematics, Engineering, Science Achievement (MESA) to the elementary level.
3. Seat those who are not performing as well closer to teachers.
4. Provide longer wait time for those not performing as well to answer questions.
5. Give those not performing as well clues or try repeating or rephrasing questions.
6. Do not criticize more often students who are not performing as well for failure.
7. Interact with students who are not performing as well more publicly than privately.
8. Use decor in classroom that is inspirational and culturally reinforcing.
9. Encourage a high level of self-respect for all students.
10. Provide equitable response opportunities for all students.
11. Maintain equitable feedback for all students.
12. Ensure that students ask more questions than the teacher.
13. Develop critical thinking skills by asking open-ended questions.
14. Implement assertive, consistent, complementary, and clearly established rules and consequences.
15. Provide cooperative learning experiences.
16. Create and enforce stipulations that if parents do not complete their school volunteer hours, their child's younger siblings will not be considered for admission.
17. Create a schoolwide atmosphere that encourages parental involvement.
18. Provide parent manuals with tips and guidelines.

Middle School

1. Assume parents care about their children and want the best for them.
2. Make positive calls to home.
3. Provide students access to computers during lunch and after-school hours.
4. Offer RTIs that support students by the best subject-matter teachers working with the students who need the most help.
5. Offer college and career readiness programs.
6. Offer dropout prevention and retrieval programs.

7. Provide rigorous curriculum with strong emphasis on STEM areas and language development.
8. Keep in mind that parents may have had bad experiences in school that serve as barriers to their involvement.
9. Hold PTAs, PTOs, and CBOs in apartment complexes, community centers, and faith-based institutions where parents feel safe.
10. Do not assume parents are literate in any language.
11. Keep in mind that in elementary school parents have one teacher to talk to; in middle school they have more than one, which can be intimidating.
12. Have someone greet parents at the door during parent teacher conferences to provide directions and a welcoming environment.
13. Facilitate parents' reading and understanding of school improvement plans.
14. Offer resume-writing class, not parental education classes.

High School

1. Provide clear curriculum choices for students.
2. Offer both remediation and acceleration courses.
3. Provide wraparound student support.
4. Be responsible for providing easily accessible adult support.
5. Facilitate opportunities that involve the whole family.
6. Offer a clear and deep focus on college preparation.
7. Demystify the college-going experience for students and parents.
8. Articulate a transparent and outlined initiative of reforms, specifically targeting the persistence of an achievement gap.
9. Utilize frequent assessments of student progress and multiple opportunities for improvement.
10. Employ an emphasis on nonfiction writing.
11. Encourage collaborative scoring of student work.
12. Deliver a rigorous curriculum.
13. Provide a clear and deep focus on academic achievement.
14. Offer real-world experiences that have cultural relevance.
15. Reduce student-to-teacher ratios whenever you can.
16. Identify students who are not at proficiency based on NEAP and intervene early utilizing the subject-matter teachers for classroom prep before class or after class.

17. Document by log which group/individual is helping which student so that all intervention is data driven.
18. Keep in mind that student interest and homework completion wanes depending on the time of the school year.
19. Know where student is at in regards to GPA and classes they need to take to stay on track for graduation.
20. Empower principals to be instructional leaders.
21. Teach for mastery.
22. Encourage and support teacher collaboration.
23. Hire teachers who hold themselves accountable.
24. Utilize targeted professional development.
25. Create a climate where teachers value professional learning.
26. Employ continuous improvement strategies.
27. Make sound fiscal decisions.

Effective Teacher Self Survey

■ **DESCRIPTION.** The phrase 'high expectations' is synonymous with teacher effectiveness. However, even the best intentioned and most knowledgeable teachers often wonder how to implement high expectations successfully in the classroom.

■ **OBJECTIVES.** To offer teachers a guide that can help begin internal self-reflection and external dialogue with colleagues in a way that takes this popular phrase into concrete teaching strategies.

■ **OUTCOMES.** A handy resource to inform pedagogy to close achievement gaps for African American males.

■ **DIRECTIONS.**
1. Fill out the self-survey honestly.
2. Look over the *survey and decipher any trends.*
3. Use the survey trends to adapt your teaching strategies.

1. Today did I maintain an overall atmosphere (verbal and nonverbal) of general encouragement and support for learning in process of all students? **Y / N**
2. Today did I get to know parents or guardians of the children in my classrooms? **Y / N**
3. Today did I maintain an orderly environment that is safe, structured, and comfortable? **Y / N**
4. Today did I remember that I am not expected to be a social worker, but that I am expected to know when to refer children to support personnel such as social workers and/or psychologists? **Y / N**
5. Today did I remember that some children are homeless and live in shelters at night and sometimes attend multiple schools during the year? **Y / N**
6. Today did I not only have high expectations but also set clear standards of attainable academic and behavioral performance and hold students to them? **Y / N**
7. Today did I carefully think, plan, and make decisions to ensure strategic teaching? **Y / N**
8. Today did I call on all students to participate in classroom discussion with challenging questions, in multiple forms, related to the cognitive information being covered? **Y / N**
9. Today did I give students adequate time to formulate answers when called upon? **Y / N**
10. Today did I help to lead students into correct answers using encouragement and clues, and by developing and shaping answers interactively: probe, restate questions, give hints, etc.? reinforce good responses in multiple ways? **Y / N**

11. Today did I structure opportunities for students to achieve significant success by assuring that cognitive entry is attained, by breaking down tasks, by ordered sequencing, and by using a mastery learning model that includes presentation, guided practice, independent practice, review assessment, reinstruction, and reinforcement? **Y / N**

12. Today did I react to student responses with praise at the appropriate time in the appropriate amount? **Y / N**

13. Today did I remember to use significant amounts of positive nonverbal behavior, such as smiling, nodding positively, looking students directly in the eye, leaning orward, and encouraging more than one direct response? **Y / N**

14. Today did I design learning activities to be challenging, engaging, relevant, and directed to student motivations? **Y / N**

15. Today did I remember to be proactively available; did I actively assist students and demonstrate willingness to help during both class and nonclass time; and did I encourage students we are "response-reticent"? **Y / N**

16. Today did I give adequate evaluative feedback and constructive criticism that are, and are perceived as, positive and instructional? **Y / N**

17. Today did I place primary stress on academic role definition, and not settle for solely social or other nonacademic goals? **Y / N**

18. Today did I get to know the culture and background of my students, not to use it as an excuse for failure, but to understand the culture to use positive aspects of that to propel student achievement? **Y / N**

19. Today did I appreciate and celebrate diversity in the classroom? **Y / N**

20. Today did I update my skills in some way? **Y / N**

21. Today did I participate in induction, mentoring, or collaborative activities with experienced teachers? **Y / N**

Dropout Factors

■ **DESCRIPTION.** Keeping up with emerging trends and directions surrounding dropout rates can be challenging. Having a resource guide to help navigate turbulent educational outcomes waters may be beneficial.

■ **OBJECTIVES.** To help parents, teachers' administrators and stakeholders increase their capacity to successfully decrease dropouts.

■ **OUTCOMES.** A better understanding of the complex issue of dropout prevention.

■ **DIRECTIONS.**
1. Make note of what you are of and what you were not aware of.
2. Work to improve the areas you can and seek help for the areas you cannot.

Academic Student Experiences

1. Could not keep up with studies
2. Couldn't get along with other students
3. Failing classes
4. Poor grades/lack of ability/low achievement
5. Thought could not complete course requirements
6. Thought would fail competency test
7. Friends were dropping out/peer pressure
8. Had wanted to quit as soon as I could legally
9. Thought it would be easier to get a GED
10. Could not afford a four-year education
11. Didn't like school/school was not for me
12. Felt like I didn't belong
13. Moved to another city/changed schools and didn't like new one
14. Some people in school thought I was a juvenile delinquent

Non-Academic Student Experiences

15. Had a drug or alcohol problem
16. Became pregnant

17. Employment/had to work/wanted to work
18. Enlisted in the armed forces/Wanted to enlist
19. Financial reasons
20. Gang activity
21. Had a baby/became parent
22. Planned to get married or got married
23. Poor health/illness
24. The job I wanted did not require more schooling
25. Wanted to have a family
26. Wanted to travel

Demographics

27. Family obligations
28. Financial difficulties at home
29. Had to care for a family member
30. Had to support family/self
31. Home responsibilities
32. Lack of parental support

School Factors

33. Could not get along with teachers
34. Minimum competency requirements too difficult
35. Missed too many school days
36. Rigorous academic standards are too difficult
37. School was too dangerous/was not safe
38. Suspended/expelled
39. Was expelled/was about to be expelled
40. Didn't get into desired program
41. Low student expectations for payoff to education

Instructional Practices

42. Low teacher expectations for student performance

Digital Native vs. Digital Immigrant Teacher Survey

■ **DESCRIPTION.** Occasionally teachers use technology unconsciously or as an accessory to learning. Many teachers have asked us how to incorporate technology into their teaching practices more methodically. Here is a good place to start.

■ **OBJECTIVES.** To help identify areas that can be used to improve the way teachers can consciously use technology in a way that increases student engagement, learning, and achievement.

■ **OUTCOME.** Increased capacity to successfully use an objective and informal self-assessment tool to improve technology use in the classroom.

■ **DIRECTIONS.**
1. Fill out the chart to the best of your knowledge.
2. Score the assessment based on the coding below.
3. Use the assessment to identify items you would like to improve and re-take the survey every three months to gauge improvement. (Feel free to make changes.)

	NEVER	RARELY	OCCASIONALLY	OFTEN	ALWAYS
1. I regularly use a computer as part of my teaching practice.	①	②	③	④	⑤
2. I regularly use a SMARTboard as part of my teaching practice.	①	②	③	④	⑤
3. I regularly use smartphones as part of my teaching practice.	①	②	③	④	⑤
4. I regularly use tablets/chrome books as part of my teaching practice.	①	②	③	④	⑤

5. I integrate technology as part of my teaching practice.

   ①   ②   ③   ④   ⑤

6. I integrate technology as part of homework assignments.

   ①   ②   ③   ④   ⑤

7. I feel that my school supports my use of technology.

   ①   ②   ③   ④   ⑤

8. Is lack of resources among your students in accessing digital technologies a "major challenge" to you incorporating more digital tools into your teaching?

   ①   ②   ③   ④   ⑤

   NEVER   **RARELY**   **OCCASIONALLY**   **OFTEN**   **ALWAYS**

9. I regularly use education-friendly websites as part of my teaching practice.

   ①   ②   ③   ④   ⑤

10. I help students outside of class time.

    ①   ②   ③   ④   ⑤

11. I make time to help students outside of the school schedule (i.e., evenings and weekends).

    ①   ②   ③   ④   ⑤

    NOT AT ALL   **NOT VERY**   **SOMEWHAT**   **MOSTLY**   **VERY**

12. I am comfortable using computers in the classroom.

    ①   ②   ③   ④   ⑤

13. I am comfortable using educational technology in the classroom.

    ①   ②   ③   ④   ⑤

14. My school provides formal training on how to use digital technology to enhance instruction.

    ①   ②   ③   ④   ⑤

15. I feel that I am adequately exposed to new trends and directions in education technology.

    ①   ②   ③   ④   ⑤

■ **CODING**

15–57	Digital Immigrant	70–75 Digital Native
58–63	Researching and Learning	
64–69	Becoming Naturalized	

Stone Age ⟶ Digital Age

High Expectations, Black Males, and Digital Technology

- **OBJECTIVES.**
  - To help the teacher examine his or her beliefs about high expectations.
  - To increase understanding surrounding Black males.
  - To facilitate interactive, digital classrooms for twenty-first-century learners.

- **OUTCOMES.** Participants will:
  - Increase knowledge of new trends and directions of research surrounding high expectations.
  - Amplify capacity for working with African American young males.
  - Create strategies that build engaging and interactive digital classrooms.

- **ACTIVITIES.** Meaningful conversations, exercises, and strategies in both small and large groups.

- **GUIDED QUESTIONS.**
  - How are you using technology to raise expectations of *at-risk* students?
  - Are you meeting the expectations of your Black male students?
  - Are your classroom digital resources aligned with the way twenty-first-century learners learn?

- **REFLECTION STRATEGIES.**
  - As you think about today's activities, what does high expectations mean to you and what does it look like in the classroom?
  - As you reflect on the day's activities, what strategies will you use to foster a better understanding of Black males in a way that empowers them?
  - As you consider today's activities, what strategies will you use to make your classroom more student directed (SOLE) vs. teacher directed?

- **SESSION OUTLINE.**
Part 1. Video Clip Reflection Exercise. Watch both of the video clips below and choose one from the following section.
Watch both:
  - 10 Expectations—3:02 min. https://www.youtube.com/watch?v=K96c-TGnSf4 (posted by Leaving ToLearn.org)

- Best Practices for Teaching African American Boys—5:36 min. https://www.youtube.com/watch?v=DeUFhei81wg (posted by Knowledge Delivery Systems at www.kdsi.org)

Choose from one of the following:

- Digital Natives vs. Digital Immigrants IST 110—4:56 min (LoL at 3:00 min.), https://www.youtube.com/watch?v=ohXZ4wlekRg (available on YouTube.com)
- Future of Learning Mitra Cut: Sugata Mitra, winner of the 2013 TED Prize, discusses the future of learning, self-organized learning environment (SOLE)—5:45 min. https://www.youtube.com/watch?v=xNzt_xaVYao (available on YouTube.com)
- Smartphones in Schools—2:06 min. https://www.youtube.com/watch?v=suO4FKuzCE4 (posted by Richard de Meij at CelebrateLanguages.com)
- Mozaik—Innovative Education Solutions 9:03 min. https://www.youtube.com/watch?v=YQ8Xzqe67zM (Posted by Mozaik Education at www.mozaLearn.com)

Part 2. Discussion Exercise. Discuss in teams of at least three in a team for 10–20 minutes:

- Fostering high expectations.
- Understanding Black males and education.
- Using technology to support learning.
- Incorporating technology in the classroom

Part 3. Poster Exercise. Create a poster on 3M Easel Pad Post-it Paper, 30 minutes:

- Post the posters around the room for others to share in a gallery walk.
- Give everyone a sticky dot to place their favorite ideas on each poster.

■ **SUMMARY AND CONCLUDING THOUGHTS.** Discuss what ideas and/or strategies participants thought were the most interesting.

RTI Teacher Implementation Survey

■ **DESCRIPTION.** Not all teachers are aware of the potential of RTI.

■ **OBJECTIVES.** To help teachers pinpoint stumbling RTI blocks they may not have been aware of.

■ **OUTCOMES.** A better understanding how you utilize RTI in your teaching practice.

■ **DIRECTIONS.**
1. Fill out the self-survey honestly.
2. Use the survey trends to make professional development recommendations.

1. I understand the difference between RTI and special education.   Y / N
2. I believe that RTI can be used to help uncover behavioral problems for students who are not being challenged enough.   Y / N
3. I am aware that RTI is also helpful for students who are high achieving.   Y / N
4. I understand that RTI placements are based on specified student achievement data.   Y / N
5. I feel that I have had enough training to teach RTI-driven lessons.   Y / N
6. I feel that my principal and I are on the same page regarding RTI.   Y / N
7. I feel that I have the resources and materials needed to successfully implement RTI.   Y / N
8. I feel that I have the support needed to successfully implement RTI.   Y / N
9. I feel that parents are aware of our current RTI program.   Y / N
10. I believe that RTI can play a crucial role in closing the achievement gap.   Y / N
11. I feel that my colleagues understand and support RTI as a method for closing the achievement gap.   Y / N

RTI Effective Teacher Survey

■ **DESCRIPTION.** Not all teachers feel supported using RTI.

■ **OBJECTIVES.** To help evaluate the hard work that your teachers do to facilitate response to intervention.

■ **OUTCOMES.** A better understanding how teachers view and feel supported using RTI.

■ **DIRECTIONS.**
1. Have your evaluator fill out the survey.
2. Use the survey trends to structure future professional development strategies.

	STRONGLY AGREE	AGREE	NEUTRAL	DISAGREE	STRONGLY DISAGREE
1. Did the teacher implement differentiated instruction based on student achievement data?	①	②	③	④	⑤
2. Does the teacher regularly update and reassess benchmark levels?	①	②	③	④	⑤
3. Has the teacher been given the resources and training needed to implement changes?	①	②	③	④	⑤
4. Do teachers provide opportunities for students with similar issues to work in groups?	①	②	③	④	⑤
5. Is the principal the instructional leader of the school?	①	②	③	④	⑤
6. Does the teacher try to adapt to the students' learning style?	①	②	③	④	⑤
7. Does the school climate or district policies promote data-driven differentiated learning practices?	①	②	③	④	⑤
8. Does school/district leadership meet regularly to evaluate data-driven differentiated instruction?	①	②	③	④	⑤
9. Does the school/district offer continuous professional development for its teachers?	①	②	③	④	⑤

Common Core Implementation Survey

■ **DESCRIPTION.** Many educators have expressed interest into how to seamlessly integrate Common Core into the classroom.

■ **OBJECTIVES.** To offer educators a self-assessment survey that can be used to pinpoint areas that may need more support.

■ **OUTCOMES.** A handy resource that can begin conversation to improve teaching practices.

■ **DIRECTIONS.**
1. Fill out the survey below honestly.
2. Use the survey trends as a starting place to seek additional support.

Use this survey as a self-assessment of your knowledge of Common Core.

1. I understand the relationship of Common Core and RTI.   Y / N
2. I am aware that Common Core standards are also helpful for students who
   re high achieving.   Y / N
3. I understand that Common Core standards are based on specified student
   achievement data.   Y / N
4. I feel that I have had enough training to teach lessons based on Common Core.   Y / N
5. I feel that my principal and I are on the same page regarding Common Core.   Y / N
6. I feel that I have the resources and materials needed to successfully implement
   Common Core.   Y / N
7. I feel that I have the support needed to successfully implement Common Core.   Y / N
8. I feel that parents are aware of Common Core standards.   Y / N
9. I believe that Common Core standards can play a crucial role in closing the
   achievement gap.   Y / N
10. I feel that my colleagues understand and support Common Core standards
    as a method for closing the achievement gap.   Y / N

Mentorship Implementation Plan

■ **DESCRIPTION.** Program planners often seek concrete ways to collect quantitative and qualitative data to evaluative the effectiveness of their mentorship programs.

■ **OBJECTIVES.** To help the program planners determine which areas of their mentorship programs need improvement.

■ **OUTCOMES.** This form will help program planners design better mentorship programs through analyzing data.

■ **DIRECTIONS.**
1. Devise a plan on how to collect data on the mentorship program.
2. Collect data.
3. Develop an improvement plan for the program.

Qualitative and Quantitative Data

MENTORS
- Race
- Gender
- Age
- Career
- Educational Level
- Time Spent in the Program
- Satisfaction

MENTEES' ACADEMIC/CAREER PROGRESS
- Improvement in Pre-Test Scores
- Improvement in Post-Test Scores
- Contact Hours
- Teachers' Comments on Behavioral and Academic Progress
- Increase in Report Cards Grades
- Career Obtainment
- Graduation Obtainment
- Postsecondary Enrollment

PROGRAM

- Retention Rates
- Source of Mentors
- Mentor Evaluations from the Supervisor
- Advisory Committee's Evaluations (quarterly)
- Stakeholders' Perceptions of the Program
- Parent Surveys
- SMART Goals Attainment
- Entry Surveys
- Exit Surveys
- Evaluations by the Mentee
- Evaluations by the Mentor
- Duration of the Mentorship Relationship
- Mentor Attendance
- Mentee Attendance
- Mentor/Mentor Combinations (race and gender)

MENTEES

- Race
- Gender
- Educational Level
- Family Demographics
- Mentor Name
- Time Spent in the Program
- Satisfaction
- Increase in Positive Attitude Towards School
- Increase in Positive Attitude Towards Life
- Decrease in Behavioral Problems
- Decrease in Discipline Referrals
- Improvement in Self-Esteem
- Decrease in Suspensions
- Decrease in School Requested Parent Conferences
- Decrease in Dropouts
- Decrease Recidivism
- Decrease in Absenteeism
- Decrease in Truancy

Teacher Mentee Evaluation Survey

■ **DESCRIPTION.** Not everyone is aware that mentorship is more than just showing up and talking but something that can be assessed.

■ **OBJECTIVES.** To help teachers and mentors pinpoint areas that should be maintained or improved with mentee/mentor interactions.

■ **OUTCOMES.** A better understanding of how mentee/mentor interactions have a direct and measurable impact in the classroom.

■ **DIRECTIONS.**

1. Have the mentee's teacher(s) fill out the survey.
2. Adapt mentor sessions based on trends that should be sustained or that can be improved.
3. Re-administer the survey after three months.
4. See if any improvements correlate to time spent with your student's mentor.

	VERY UNLIKELY	SOMEWHAT UNLIKELY	NO CHANGE NEUTRAL	SOMEWHAT LIKELY	VERY LIKELY
1. How likely are you to say that your mentee has improved in reading so far this year?	①	②	③	④	⑤
2. How likely are you to say that your mentee has improved in math so far this year?	①	②	③	④	⑤
3. How likely are you to say that your mentee is behaving better in class so far this year?	①	②	③	④	⑤
4. How likely are you to say that your mentee has increased both his social capital and his academic capital?	①	②	③	④	⑤

_____   _____   _____

MENTEE NAME   TEACHER SIGNATURE   DATE

Increasing Positive Responses to Expectation Violations Handout

■ **DESCRIPTION.** Many behavioral interaction problems in the classroom are based on student comprehension issues and teacher frustration.

■ **OBJECTIVES.** To build upon or increase help-seeking behavior in ways that affirm the identity of male students of color.

■ **OUTCOMES.** An increased awareness of how to identify positive responses to expectation violations and knowledge of how to create and implement behavioral intervention plans specifically tailored to individual students.

■ **DIRECTIONS.**
1. Look over the example below.
2. Fill out the blank form using the provided example to model your own classroom observations.
3. Create a strategy and objective that improves teacher-student relationships.

■ **SAMPLE.**

SITUATION: Very specific; who, what, when, where, why, and how.	On Thursday in Dr. Ransaw's room during a lecture about medical care costs.
BEHAVIOR: List actions only, no judgments and lots of verbs; i.e., tone of voice, body language, word choice, etc.	James and Ryan (students) stopped following along during class to open their smart phone browsers.
EXPECTATION VIOLATION: The consequence of the behavior on the audience.	Because James and Ryan were not paying attention they could miss pertinent information regarding the test, encourage other students to not pay attention, were a distraction to Dr. Ransaw, and violated the class's cell phone use expectation.

STRATEGY: *Probe for more information.* Instead of assuming James and Ryan were being intentionally disruptive, Dr. Ransaw gently reminded them about the no cell phone in class rule. James and Ryan apologized to Dr. Ransaw and told him that one of them was looking up how much the local hospital charged for overnight medical stay and additional fees while the other was adding up the total. They shared with the class their information and helped to enhance Dr. Ransaw's national stats with local figures. Dr. Ransaw changed the smartphone policy in class by making them part of the learning experience.

OUTCOME: By creating opportunities for students to use their smartphones as part of the lesson and during class at appropriate times, Dr. Ransaw increased both student engagement and retention.

SITUATION: Very specific; who, what, when, where, why, and how.	
BEHAVIOR: List actions only, no judgments and lots of verbs; i.e., tone of voice, body language, word choice, etc.	
EXPECTATION VIOLATION: The consequence of the behavior on the audience.	

STRATEGY:
OUTCOME:

Tips for Making School Cool

■ **WHERE DID COOL COME FROM?** The concept of cool has been traced back to Africa (Janzen, 1972). In fact, the word "cool" stems from *ewuare*, a Yoruba term in West Africa that is often assigned to one who is crowned king (Majors & Billson, 1992). Cool in Africa is associated with attributes such as patience and mental calmness and is often expressed through art, dance rituals, and, most importantly, competitive environments such as elite, all-male warrior cults (Thompson, 1984).

■ **WHAT IS COOL?** Cool intersects every aspect of race, class, and gender (Wilkins, 2008). Cool can be displayed not only in action and identity formation but in speech as well as dress (Kirkland & Jackson, 2009). Connor (1995) asserts that coolness can be a form of resilience and strength.

■ **WHY IS COOL SO IMPORTANT TO STUDENTS?** Students today are often faced with two choices in the classroom: to be popular or to be smart (Kunjufu, 1988). Being too smart is considered acting nerdy, and being dumb is just that, dumb (Ransaw, 2013). The most popular kid in class is rarely the smartest. Somewhere along the way, being smart became associated with not being popular. This balancing act, between being social and being a scholar, is an attempt to find a "middle way" between schoolwork and "cool work" (Frosh, Phoenix, & Pattman, 2002, 205).

■ **WHY IS COOL IMPORTANT TO TEACHERS?** Many African American males feel that school is not a welcoming place. As a result, they portray themselves in a way that affirms their masculine identity, described as the *cool pose* (Majors & Billson, 1992). Cool pose is the masculine appearance of being   resilient, relaxed, confident, and emotionally detached (Hecht, Jackson, & Ribeau, 2003). However, this cool pose can be misinterpreted as lack of engagement and disinterest by educators (Ransaw, 2013).

■ **IS COOL JUST AN AFRICAN AMERICAN MALE THING?** No. In fact, the art of masking emotions in Spanish, especially among young Latino males, is called *la cara de palo* or "wooden mask" (De La Cancela, 1994, p. 33). Being straight-faced as well as not appearing weak is a construct of many forms of masculinity (Bean & Ransaw, 2013). Avoiding being perceived as socially inept is more than just a form of social capital; it is also a matter of survival to escape being bullied (Frosh et al., 2002).

■ **WHAT CAN I DO TO HELP MAKE SCHOOL COOL?**

Use Cool Technology

When students come to school, we ask them to turn off their cell phones, shut down their laptops, and tune in to learning. In short, we ask them to unplug. However, most students are digital natives fluent in the use of technology, and we as teachers are mostly digital immigrants, not hardwired to use technology. Today's student uses technology to learn in new ways we may not realize. Using technology in the classroom is natural to them, so why not let them (Brown & Fox, 2013)?

RESOURCES

Ian Jukes, "Teaching the Digital Generation: Powerful Teaching"

Tom Chatfield, "7 ways video games engage the brain"

"K–12 Education: Connecting to a Digital Generation"

Make Reading Cool

Theodore Ransaw found that students will read and understand if you give them text that has meaning in their lives. For example, it *is* possible to engage boys in reading by utilizing multifaceted texts that affirm their identity (Bean & Ransaw, 2013). Use *enabling text* that moves beyond a solely cognitive focus—such as skill and strategy development—to include a social, cultural, political, spiritual, or economic focus" (Tatum, 2008, p. 164).

RESOURCES

• *K–12*

The Boy who Harnessed the Wind, by William Kamkwamba and Bryan Mealer, illustrated by Elizabeth Zunon (New York: Dial Books, 2012).

Goal Line, by Tiki Barber and Ronde Barber with Paul Mantell (New York: Simon & Schuster, 2011).

• *ELEMENTARY*

An Inside Look at the U.S. Navy SEALs, by Joe Funk (New York: Scholastic, 2011).

We Are the Ship: The Story of Negro League Baseball, words and paintings by Kadir Nelson (Mattituck, NY: Amereon House, 1992).

• *JR. HIGH*

Bad Boy: A Memoir, by Walter Dean Myers (New York: Harper Collins, 2001).

Ain't Nothing But a Man: My Quest to Find the Real John Henry, by Scott Reynolds Nelson with Marc Aronson (Washington, DC: National Geographic, 2008).

• *HIGH SCHOOL*

You Don't Even Know Me: Stories and Poems about Boys, by Sharon Flake (New York: Jump at the

Sun, 2010).

First Crossing: Stories about Teenage Immigrants, ed. by Donald R. Gallo (Cambridge, MA: Candlewick Press, 2004).

Make Science Cool

Christopher Emdin created Science Genius to help students see themselves as scientists. Science Genius started as a way to engage students from ten New York City High Schools through hip-hop. Dr. Edmin and a few of his graduate students worked with one class per school, one day per week, to teach basic science concepts. The high school students then had a science rap battle that went from best in class, to best in school, to best in city. The winner got to call himself a Science Genius for a year. Attendance for the year increased. "Kids relate best when they're standing up," Edmin notes. "The teacher can measure engagement by the hand gestures and head bobs. And when the last kid couldn't finish his verse, everybody gave him encouragement. In a traditional school, he'd have failed. We need to expand the notion of what success is" (Emdin, 2014).

RESOURCES

Science Genius, http://rapgenius.com/artists/Science-genius

Dr. Christopher Emdin, http://chrisemdin.com

National Geographic Learning / Cengage Learning, http://ngl.cengage.com

Make Math Cool

Algebra Project was founded by Dr. Robert Moses (Moses & Cobb, 2001) and has had great success using culturally adaptive norms to improve young African Americans' advanced mathematics capabilities. This work is especially important since research suggests that enrolling in Algebra I by eighth grade is an indicator for success in college for minorities (Oakes, Joseph, & Muir, 2004). By taking students on a subway train, often decorated with graffiti, Moses was able to engage in conversations with them using language they used in their own environment to make parallels in mathematics. A subway train route became a metaphor for a number line; stops along the way took the place of numbers on the number line (Moses & Cobb, 2001). If, for example, a subway train goes forward five stops (positive five) than goes back two stops (negative two) how far has it gotten?

RESOURCES

Kakooma, online math game site, http://GregTangMath.com/kakooma

Formula Learn, smartphone application for student/teacher math help, https://itunes.apple.

com/us/app/formula-learn/id693391470?mt=8

Math Dictionary for Kids, by T. F. Fitzgerald (Waco: Prufrock Press under NCTM Review, 2011).

REFERENCES

Bean, T. W., & Ransaw, T. (2013). Masculinity and portrayals of African-American boys in young adult literature: A critical deconstruction and reconstruction of this genre. In B. J. Guzzetti and T. W. (Eds.), *Adolescent literacies and the gendered self: (Re)constructing identities through multimodal literacy practices*. New York: Routledge.

Brown, N., & Fox, M. (2013). *Digital differences: The "haves" and the "have-nots."* Afternoon breakout session, Coaching 101. Dearborn, MI.

Connell, R. W. (1995). *Masculinities*. Cambridge: Polity Press.

Connell, R. W. (1996). Teaching the boys: New research on masculinity, and gender strategies for schools. *Teachers College Record 98*(2), 206–235.

Connor, M. K. (1995). *What is cool? Understanding Black manhood in America*. New York: Crown.

De La Cancela, V. (1994). "Coolin": The psychosocial communication of African and Latino men. In D. J. Jones (Ed.), *African American males: A critical link in the African American family* (pp. 33–45). New Brunswick: Transaction Publishers.

Frosh, S., Phoenix, A., & Pattman, R. (2002). *Young masculinities: Understanding boys in contemporary society*. Basingstoke: Palgrave.

Hecht, M. L., Jackson, R. L., & Ribeau, S. A. (2003). *African American communication: Exploring identity and culture* (2nd ed.). Mahwah, NJ: Lawrence Erlbaum Associates.

Janzen, J. M. (1972). Laman's Kongo ethnography: Observations on sources, methodology, and theory. *Africa 42*, 316–328.

Kirkland, D. (2013). *African American male learning styles*. African American Young Men of Promise Initiative. Lansing: Michigan Department of Education

Kirkland, D. E., & Jackson, A. (2009). "We real cool": Toward a theory of black masculine literacies. *Reading Research Quarterly 44*, 278–297.

Kunjufu, J. (1988). *To be popular or smart: The Black peer group*. Chicago: African American Images.

Leland, J. (2012). A Hip-Hop Experiment. *New York Times*.

Majors, R., & Billson, J. M. (1992). *Cool pose: The dilemmas of Black manhood in America*. New York: Lexington Books.

Moses, R. P., & Cobb, C. E. (2001). *Radical equations: Math literacy and civil rights*. Boston: Beacon Press.

Oakes, J., Joseph, R., & Muir, K. (2004). Access and achievement in mathematics and science: Inequalities that endure and change. In J. A. Banks & C. A. McGee-Banks (Eds.), *Handbook of research in multicultural education* (2nd ed.), 69–90. San Francisco: Jossey-Bass.

Ransaw, T. S. (2013). *The art of being cool: The pursuit of Black masculinity.* Chicago: African American Images.

Tatum, A. W. (2005). *Teaching reading to Black adolescent males: Closing the achievement gap.* Portland, ME: Stenhouse.

Tatum, A. W. (2008). Toward a more anatomically complete model of literacy instruction: A focus on African American male adolescents and texts. *Harvard Educational Review, 78,* 155–180.

Thompson, R. F. (1984). *Flash of the spirit: African and Afro-American art and philosophy.* New York: Random House.

Wilkins, A. C. (2008). *Wannabes, goths, and Christians: The boundaries of sex, style, and status.* Chicago: University of Chicago Press.

Contributors

Charesha Barrett has more than ten years of experience in K–12 and higher education. She has a bachelor of science degree in education with a minor in history from the University of Akron. In addition, Barrett beholds two graduate degrees from Cleveland State University in supervision and in adult learning and development. She has extensive experience in facilitating professional development workshops for teachers and participating in educational leadership committees. Barrett is passionate about getting involved in education advocacy in order to narrow the achievement gap through collaborating with stakeholders on the development of college- and career-readiness and family and community engagement programs.

Stephen Brown currently serves as director in the Student Services Division at Mount San Antonio College in Walnut, California. He has taught masters-level social work courses at Azusa Pacific University and California State University Los Angeles, and undergraduate courses at Chapman University. Brown has extensive experience in the areas of foster care and adoptions. His professional work experiences include program directorship of a Los Angeles area foster family agency, program coordination of the Family Preservation with the Pomona Unified School, and child welfare practice with the Los Angeles and San Bernardino Counties Departments of Children's Services and residential treatment facilities. In addition, he acts a consultant/trainer for a number of agencies throughout the Los Angeles area and the Inland Empire. He has also provided field supervision for students from the Schools of Social Work at the University of Southern California and California State University, Los Angeles. He holds a Doctor of Education Organizational Leadership from the University of La Verne, and a master of social work degree, as well as a bachelor of science degree in psychology from Jackson State University.

Jonathan J. Doll is an educationalist, advocate, and dropout researcher from Hamburg, New York. His work includes the 2015 book, *Ending School Shootings: School and District Tools for Prevention and Action.* He was also successful in researching a World War II veteran and helping that man reunite with a family that he had lost contact with fifty-nine years earlier during the time of the war. His bachelor's degree was in math education, leading to his teaching career in math, journalism, and every other subject that his principals needed. His master's degree was in Curriculum and Instruction from the University of Alaska, where he studied the impact of affirming Alaska Native culture in the classroom. The research project titled "Come On In: An Epic Story of an Inupiat Couple in Northwestern Alaska" is on file in the Rare Books Collection at the University of Alaska in Fairbanks. Finally, his doctorate of philosophy was attained from Texas A&M University, where his dissertation was on teachers' and administrators' perceptions of the antecedents of school dropout among English language learners at selected Texas schools. He has also recently authored an article on understanding trend changes in school dropout over the last forty-five years.

Kevin K. Green currently works at EOIR Technologies as a computer vision scientist and project lead in the Advanced Research Group Division with a focus on computer vision technology. He has more than twenty-four years of engineering research and development experience, and he has earned electrical engineering degrees from George Washington University (BSEE), the University of Michigan (MSEE), and the University of South Florida (Ph.D.). Among his publications are "Best Practices on How Teachers Can Instill Confidences and Competence in Math Students," a chapter in *Expectations in Education: Readings on High Expectations, Effective Teaching, and Student Achievement,* edited by Robert L. Green (2009) and a co-authorship of the 2014 Scholastic publication *Expect the Most—Provide the Best,* a book that explores how high expectations, innovation, and digital technology can reduce achievement gaps. Green is an entrepreneur whose company specializes in developing mobile and web online tutoring tools.

Robert L. Green is Dean and Professor Emeritus and Distinguished Alumnus at Michigan State University. He is a scholar and activist on issues related to urban schools and educational equity. He is the author of many books and reports on education issues. Over the past forty years, he has provided consulting services to more than twenty-five school districts. He is currently working with the Grand Rapids Public Schools in Grand Rapids, Michigan. In this book, he has applied knowledge from work on behalf of Michigan State University and school districts in Dallas, Portland, Detroit, Memphis, and San Francisco. During his career, he created staff development strategies for teachers and administrators and produced research and initiatives to help reform schools, close achievement gaps, and improve graduation rates. He is a leader in academic performance monitoring and assessment, and he develops strategies to improve student performance at every level.

Richard Majors, a former clinical fellow in psychology at Harvard Medical School, is currently the director and a senior fellow of the Applied Centre of Emotional Literacy Leadership and Research. He is a counselling psychologist and a visiting professor at the University of Colorado in the United States, who has been working in the UK for more than ten years. His book *Cool Pose*, which is considered a classic in the field, was submitted for Pulitzer Prize by the publisher and was on the publisher's best sellers list in 1992. He also is the author of *Educating Our Black Children* (2001). Dr. Majors is the founder and former editor of the *Journal of African American Men* (now the *Journal of African American Studies*). His research has been translated into several languages. He taught a short course on gender at Cambridge University. Recently, he wrote the lead psychological expert statement in the UK high court for the landmark cornrow case SG vs St. Gregory's Science School, which successfully overturned previous policy and legislation that prevented Black children from being able to wear cornrows and braids in UK schools. Dr. Majors received a Warrior award from the International Colloquium on Black Males in Education for his global contribution and leadership of and for Black males.

Mikel D. C. Moss is a drama therapist researcher in training. He is currently pursuing his studies with interests in the development of new forms of empirically supported, quantitative data-driven drama therapeutic techniques. He specifically is looking at ways to develop and support through drama therapy the areas of emotion regulation and emotional literacy in populations in the African diaspora (adolescent and young adults) dealing with depression, anxiety, post-traumatic stress disorder, and post-traumatic slave syndrome utilizing Sanford Meisners repetition exercise as an embodied form of cognitive behavior therapy.

Theodore S. Ransaw is the equity specialist for K–12 Outreach at Michigan State University's College of Education. He has publications on African American fatherhood, Black males and educational outcomes, culture- and gender-relevant literacy, as well as Black male literacy. Ransaw is a national guest speaker on issues related to Black males and literacy. He has extensive expertise in elementary mentorship for males of color and Latino and African American girls. Ransaw is also a certified education coach and legal consultant on masculinity and education. He teaches classes on diversity, masculinity, criminal justice, and Afro-American music and culture.

Sean Williams is the student instructional services supervisor for the Ingham County Intermediate School District in Michigan and the former program coordina-tor of the Michigan Fellowship of Instructional Leaders program, which is based out of the Office of K–12 Outreach at Michigan State University. Dr. Williams works with school principals to develop their abilities to design and implement substantive initiatives to improve student achievement. He is an expert in multitiered support systems and school district-wide implementation. Before joining the Office of K–12 Outreach, Williams was an award-winning classroom teacher and veteran middle school principal who transformed a low-performing school to a high-performing one in just three years. He holds a dual PhD from Michigan State University in K–12 Education Administration and Educational Policy.

Index